If I were Dictator

*a tongue-in-cheek guide
to saving our democracy*

Other books by Lisa Orban

SERIES: OKAY, PICTURE THIS...
It'll Feel Better when it Quits Hurting
Wine Comes in Six-Packs

COOKBOOK
I'd rather Starve than Cook!
A cookbook for people who hate to cookbook

VISUAL VERTIGO
Optical Illusion Coloring Books
Volume One
Volume Two
Volume Three
Volume Four

Copyright © 2018 by Lisa M. Orban

Second Edition published October 2018
Published by Indies United Publishing House, LLC

First Edition published April 1, 2018

Cover art designed by Lisa M. Orban

All rights reserved worldwide. No part of this publication may be replicated, redistributed, or given away in any form without the prior written consent of the author/publisher or the terms relayed to you herein.

ISBN 13: 978-1-64456-015-0

www.indiesunited.net

> The sale of this book without a cover is unauthorized.
> If you purchased this book without a cover, the poor Indie author who slaved over a hot computer to bring you this fine book did not receive any compensation for all of her hard work and dedication. And just so you know, every authorized book sale results in a happy dance by the author. Please, be kind, and don't deprive author of her of her happy dance just to save a few pennies.

To Chuck

A social justice warrior until the end.

If I were Dictator

a tongue-in-cheek guide
to saving our democracy

LET THE REVOLUTION BEGIN
ONE CHAPTER AT A TIME

Introduction	13
After the Revolution	15
Safeguards	17
The Constitution & Bill of Rights	19
The Media	25
Civil Forfeitures	27
CHAPTER ONE	
The Environment	**29**
Cool it Down	30
National & State Parks	32
Pipelines	34
A World of Green	36
Recycling	38
FEMA	40
CHAPTER TWO	
The Economy	**43**
Banking	45
Addressing Poverty	49
Wages	51
Away from the Grind	53
A Year of Giving	56
Universal Basic Income	58
CHAPTER THREE	
Taxes	**63**
Individual & Corporate Taxes	65
The separation of Church & State	69
Universal Basic Income - continued	70
CHAPTER FOUR	
Healthcare	**73**
Access to Care	76
Drugs & Dependency	78
The Feminine Mystique	80

CHAPTER FIVE
Education   83

    Primary School: PreK - 3rd Grade   87

    Middle School: 4th - 8th Grade   89

    Secondary School: 9th - 12th Grade   91

    Graduate School   93

CHAPTER SIX
Housing   97

    Addressing Homelessness   99

    Affordable Housing   103

    Home Ownership   106

    Revitalizing our Neighborhoods   108

CHAPTER SEVEN
Food   111

    Food Deserts   113

    Farms   116

CHAPTER EIGHT
Energy   119

    Solar & Wind   120

    A Dying Industry   123

    The Grid   125

CHAPTER NINE
Infrastructure   127

    Roads & Bridges   129

    Water & Sewer   131

    Planes, Trains & Automobiles   133

    Integrating our Systems   136

    Keeping in Touch   138

CHAPTER TEN
The Military   141

    Military Contracts   142

    Our Soldiers   144

    A Call to War   147

CHAPTER ELEVEN
International Relations — 151

- The Peacekeepers — 153
- Embassies & Outreach — 156
- Seekers — 159
- Immigration — 161

CHAPTER TWELVE
Elections — 165

- The President — 168
- The House — 171
- The Senate — 173
- U.S. Supreme Court — 174
- Judgeships — 176
- Local & State Elections — 178
- The Election Committee — 179

CHAPTER THIRTEEN
Legal Stuff — 181

- Simplifying the Legal Code — 184
- Nosy Neighbor Laws — 186
- Patent Laws — 189
- Law Enforcement & Us — 191
- Prisons — 194
- Mobs & Gangs — 199

A Final Farewell — 201

About the Author — 207

Take a deep breath, here we go...

INTRODUCTION

Hello my friends,

I should probably begin with, I truly have no interest in overthrowing the government and installing myself as your dictator, I'm much too lazy for that. Instead, this book is about using humor, sarcasm, logic, and a little bit of math to discuss many of the issues facing our nation and ways we could fix them.

We've all been experiencing it. The sinking certainty our country is no longer working for us, and we no longer matter in the larger scheme of how our laws are made, or even, why they are made. Many of us no longer feel like we are a part of the American Dream of a good job, and a nice home with a white picket fence to share with our spouse and raising our kids in relative security. And, if this isn't quite your generic American Dream, feel free to take a few moments to create your own image before we continue.

The sad fact is, wages are low, employment insecurity high, living debt is out of control, and places within our country that more resemble a third world nation, than one which reflects a country with as much wealth as we possess. I read a grim factoid not too long ago, (please don't ask me where, it's been a few months, and I read a lot of articles every day, but this number stayed with me and I'm now going to share it with you) if we broke down our nation's wealth and divided equally among every man, woman, and child, we would each receive $700,000 per year. That's a lot of money.

Or, put another way, every family of four would be millionaires, with an annual combined income of 2.8 million dollars a year. Yet, most of the wealth belongs to a small handful of people at the top of the income scale. That, my friend, is income inequity in a nutshell. I'm not saying we shouldn't reward a person for working hard and doing well, but you cannot tell me out of 323.1 million Americans, only a small handful are working hard enough to justify their possessing over half of our nation's wealth. Broken down, the top 1% is in control of 43% of our nation's wealth, and next 4% in possession of an additional 29%, leaving almost nothing for the rest of us. A mere 28% to split up among 96% of Americans.

For perspective, three individuals in our country have as much wealth as the bottom half of our country, just three. That's a lot of money, so much money it's hard to even think about as an actual thing. It's easier to imagine unicorns than it is to really grasp the concept of a third of our nation's wealth under your personal control. It's enough to make a jackpot lottery winner feel poor by comparison. And, sadly, to scale next to the top .01%, they are. It's easier to image $700,000, which is why I think it affected me so much, it's a number I could fathom, it felt real.

We may not be able to image that much wealth, but we can, and we do, feel the weight of so much money concentrated among a very few. Our economy is like a building with a weak foundation supporting a statue weighing 540% more than the rest combined. Looking at it, we know it can't hold, even as the architects who built it reassure us it *will*, we know it can't. This is our country right now my friends, a house built on a shaky foundation to support something it cannot hold.

So, the question you are probably asking is, what do we do? My honest answer is, I don't know. Instead, I present to you, *If I were Dictator*, a pretend world where I am in charge and can change anything on a whim, because, well... I'm the dictator and that's what dictators do, change things to suit themselves without having to answer for it. And maybe somewhere within these pages, we can find the beginnings of a solution for all of us before this house of cards fall down on top of us.

Your humble Dictator,
Lisa

AFTER THE REVOLUTION

Day 1

The revolution happened and inspired by my words, you have all collectively supported installing me as your dictator, for six years. Yay me, yay you, we won and now I have only six years to fix everything wrong with this country before I (mostly) return things to our regularly scheduled democratic madness. The clock is ticking and it's time to begin making all the changes to turn our nation around, for all of us.

Why only six years you ask? Simple answer, it should be long enough to fix everything, yet short enough the United States shouldn't become comfortable with having a dictator. Besides, (as I mentioned before) I'm way too lazy to want to do this for the rest of my life. After six years of dealing with all of the country's woes, I'm going to be tired (maybe a little cranky) and would like to retire and enjoy the rest of my life without all the daily stress. In my opinion, only the insane would want to do this for the rest of their lives, and I may be crazy for doing this, but I am not insane.

There's a lot to do, and I will be upfront and admit, I can't do it alone, I'm going to need help. A lot of help. And here is where the rest of you come in, I'm going to need you guys, we started this revolution together and now we're all going to have to put in the hard work to make sure it wasn't for nothing. And, I'm going to need a lot of smart people, I'm going to need experts in their fields to help me tackle the millions of problems our nation has, both big and small that's too much for one person to deal with on their own. I may know a lot of facts over a multitude of subjects, but the simple fact is, I'm not an expert in most of them. I am aware of my limitations and weaknesses, and I will need your help.

I'm going to need economists, accountants, environmental scientists, doctors, a few lawyers, community organizers, and activists. I'm going to need green tech experts, and land management people, I'm going to need city planners and poverty experts. I'm going to need educational experts, historians, and diplomats. I'm going to need... ummm, why don't we just stop here, suffice to say, I need you guys. Are you ready to help me? I hope so.

It's Day 1 and I'm going to make a list of the problems we need to fix. I like lists, clearly defining something that needs to be done and the satisfaction of crossing it off when finished. And this may be the most important list I've ever made in my life. Here we go...

01. The environment. If we can't breathe, we're all dead.

02. Economy. If we can't enjoy our lives while on this earth, what's the point of any of it?

03. Taxes. Because if we don't learn to share, none of this is possible.

04. Healthcare. Because no one should lose everything because they were sick or injured.

05. Education. We need smart, capable people and the only way to get them is to educate them.

06. Housing. Because everyone needs a place to call home.

07. Food. Can't live if we can't eat.

08. Energy. Because oil isn't forever.

09. Infrastructure. Because if everything is falling apart, our country will collapse under the rot of neglect.

10. International relations. We need more friends who actually like us.

11. The military. We need to restore rational balance, and reject the shoot first and ask questions later mentality.

12. Elections. If we are going to be a nation for the people and by the people, our elections need to reflect that.

13. Legal Stuff. Everyone deserves to live in freedom and justice.

Okay, that's the list. Are you ready to tackle it with me?
Then let's begin...

SAFEGUARDS

Before we begin, we should probably discuss a few things before we get started on this revolution. First of all, this is a work of fiction, but even so, let's go ahead and pretend we're actually doing this, and to that end, we should cover all our bases. The following few sections will be dealing not so much with problem solving as much as ground rules for our revolution and what to expect. And, if at any time there is an overthrow of our government, you can use this book as a manual. Just something to have laying around the house, break glass in case of emergency, type thing. So let us proceed...

The problem with having a dictator is, generally, absolute power corrupts absolutely, and that is not what this revolution is about. Our movement about getting our country back on track the quickest way possible. You know, basically wrestling it away from the powers-that-be and handing our country back to the people, after I've made a few tweaks.

I have no love for power, in and of, itself, but I do like the idea of not wading through layers of bureaucratize that has stifled our government and hindered progress. But, if our revolution is to succeed, there does need to be a few safeguards put in place to make sure I, as your humble Dictator, do not fall in love with power for the sake of power.

So, to keep me in check (because all power needs a check of some kind) the Secret Service will be there not only to protect me from you, but to protect you from me. If I ever decide, I love power more than I love my country, it will be their duty to step in and stop me. By whatever means necessary.

Our revolution is not about one person being in power, it's about getting power back to where it belongs, to all of us, not just a small handful of lucky and/or very rich individuals who have all the say in what our government does. A brief dictatorship, such as mine, can do this much quicker than the meandering process we have now, as long as the love of power is never allowed to flourish during my reign.

So, I will put safeguards in place to ensure this never happens.

You can rest easy during my six years as Dictator I will never stray from our mutual goal of fixing our country and making it a better place for all of us. I hope this eases your mind a bit if you were feeling a bit uncomfortable about having a dictator in charge of your democracy for a few years.

Now, let's get back to the basics of governing with the next section, the Constitution and the Bill of Rights.

THE CONSTITUTION & BILL OF RIGHTS

We the People *of the United States, in Order to form a more perfect Union, establish Justice, ensure domestic Tranquility, provide for the common defense, promote the general Welfare, and secure the Blessings of Liberty to ourselves and our Posterity, do ordain and establish this Constitution for the United States of America.*

While this country will briefly be under my dictatorship, we will not be abandoning the principles of our Founding Fathers, instead, we will be embracing the spirit of what they were attempting to create all those long years ago. Life, liberty, and the pursuit of happiness for all who are within our borders.

Our nation was founded on the idea we all were created equal, and while we were off to a rocky start with slavery still allowed to flourish, the treatment of our Native populations, and for women and children of all status, colors, and creeds. That's not to say progress hasn't been made, but we have a ways to go before we can say we are all truly equal. More steps have to be taken to make the ideals of our founding fathers a reality for every man, woman, and child, regardless of age, sex, marital status, race, sexual orientation, religion or any other artificially created standard we currently have in our society.

Starting on Day One of my dictatorship, those existing prejudges will no longer be tolerated. Every law we've ever enacted in our country under any guise that takes away rights from one group to appease another will be stripped from our legal code. Any group who incites violence or hatred towards another will not be tolerated and will be judged harshly for their actions. We have free speech in our country, and we are all free to believe whatever little fantasy tickles our soul, but when those fantasies infringe on the rights of others, a line has to be drawn. Our country's first document started with the line, *We the People*, and as your Dictator, I will be upholding the dream of our Founders, *e pluribus unum*, out of many, one.

The Constitution has been the foundation for our country, since the moment we declared independence, and while we have on occasion lost our way, we have always kept this document at the heart of all we hold dear as a country. During my six year reign, it will be the vision of a more perfect union our Founding Father's gave to us I will use as the guiding principle while I am in charge of the country.

The Bill of Rights will also remain largely unchanged. But it has become the bad habit of some to embrace one amendment to the exclusion of all others in an attempt to further their own personal agenda. We cannot allow the common good to be discarded by continuing this practice. So, let's quickly go through the first ten amendments our Founding Father's thought important enough to include.

The First Amendment
Congress shall make no law respecting an establishment of religion, or prohibiting the free exercise thereof; or abridging the freedom of speech, or of the press; or the right of the people peaceably to assemble, and to petition the Government for a redress of grievances.

We will embrace the First Amendment, and uphold the principles of its intent. The government will honor the ideals of keeping our politics out of religion, and neither embrace one to the exclusion of all others nor condemn any individual or group's religious practices, provided they do not attempt to harm or subjugate others in their practices. People are allowed to peacefully assemble and air their grievances, as long as they are not used to incite violence. We need a healthy voice in the public forum and we will encourage the public to continue to engage in public discourse.

The Second Amendment
A well regulated Militia, being necessary to the security of a free State, the right of the people to keep and bear Arms, shall not be infringed.

I believe to the depths of my soul our Founding Father's would be horrified if they witnessed what has been done in the name of the Second Amendment. It was never their intent to give blanket protection to the slaughter of innocents, but to protect us from tyranny. Unfortunately, it has become the whipping post to stir up the population and allow atrocities to happen all over our nation and excuse it. I do not plan on taking all your guns away, but we have to be reasonable and put in place common sense laws to bring sanity back to our society.

To this end, I will be enacting gun sanity laws, more or less based on the same principles as owning a car. Before you can buy a gun, you will have to pass a background check and a psychiatric exam. If you are emotionally stable and do not pose a threat to society, you may go on to the next step. You will have to take a class and learn how to operate and care for a gun, and you will have to pass the class to get a license to own a gun. Once you have completed the course, you will be required to carry gun insurance. If someone is harmed or killed with one of your guns, their care, recovery, or death benefits will be covered by your insurance policy. Once a year, you will be required to renew your license, and show proof of insurance for the full prior year. And once every five years, you will be required to undergo a psychiatric evaluation and refresher course.

Our amendments are there to protect us from our worst intentions, not sanction them. It is hard to pursue life, liberty, and happiness if we're ducking bullets in our streets, schools, and homes. And no other amendment has been perverted as much as the Second since the founding of our country. It is time to restore balance and reign in the unfettered application of it. We have free speech in our country, it's in the First Amendment, but you cannot yell fire in a crowded theater, because of the public safety factor, and the same should be applied to the Second.

The Third Amendment
No Soldier shall, in time of peace be quartered in any house, without the consent of the Owner, nor in time of war, but in a manner to be prescribed by law.

This hasn't been much of an issue, so it requires little commentary. It's there because during our time as a colony, England would house their soldiers in the homes of local populations and it was frowned upon by the people they imposed on. Since we have military housing and ample funds to house our soldiers, I don't believe this will ever be an issue. But we'll keep it, just in case, to prevent any future stupidity.

The Fourth Amendment
The right of the people to be secure in their persons, houses, papers, and effects, against unreasonable searches and seizures, shall not be violated, and no Warrants shall issue, but upon probable cause, supported by Oath or affirmation, and

particularly describing the place to be searched, and the persons or things to be seized.

In recent years, our country has gotten away from this founding principle and have gone about enacting laws to circumvent it in the forms of the Patriot Act and civil forfeiture laws. If you are unfamiliar with civil forfeiture, let me take a moment to tell you about it. Civil forfeiture has given law enforcement the abilities to seize assets from individuals, even if they haven't been accused of a crime if an officer believes those assets were gained through illicit activity. But here's the rub, they don't need to *prove* the money or property they took was actually ill-gotten gain to keep it, they only have to submit they *believe* it to be so.

This has led to a rise in cash strapped police departments seizing assets from people and using them to support their departments and it's lead to a variety of behaviors that would be crimes by any other name if not committed with a badge on their chest and civil forfeiture to hide behind. And it will end. If law enforcement cannot come up with reasonable, actionable evidence of a crime, a person should not be subjected to the loss of property and/or money merely on the say-so of an individual, even if they do wear a badge.

We will return to a more reasonable and humane treatment of our citizens, and protect all of us from too much power being given to individuals or offices without proper oversight and a clear path to address a grievance if misconduct has occurred.

The Fifth Amendment

No person shall be held to answer for a capital, or otherwise infamous crime, unless on a presentment or indictment of a grand jury except in cases arising in the land or naval forces, or in the Militia, when in actual service in time of War or public danger; nor shall any person be subject for the same offense to be twice put in jeopardy of life or limb; nor shall be compelled in any criminal case to be a witness against himself, nor be deprived of life, liberty, or property, without due process of law; nor shall private property be taken for public use, without just compensation.

We will be talking more about this in Legal Stuff, but suffice to say, we need to ensure our legal system is working for us, not being used as a means to intimidate, harass, or deprive of us of our liberties wantonly or without reasonable cause.

The Sixth Amendment

In all criminal prosecutions, the accused shall enjoy the right to a speedy and public trial, by an impartial jury of the State and district wherein the crime shall have been committed, which district shall have been previously ascertained by law, and to be informed of the nature and cause of the accusation; to be confronted with the witnesses against him; to have compulsory process for obtaining witnesses in his favor, and to have the Assistance of Counsel for his defense.

We'll cover more of this in *Legal Stuff* but, I would like to touch upon assistance of counsel. We have public defenders in our country who (generally) work hard for their defendants, but they are often underfunded, underpaid, and so overworked, many who might have gone free under different circumstances, instead, end up in jail because of overworked lawyers. This is a problem we can easily solve with money, and we will work hard to correct the injustices that have been done because of the current system.

The Seventh Amendment

In suits at common law, where the value in controversy shall exceed twenty dollars, the right of trial by jury shall be preserved, and no fact tried by a jury, shall be otherwise re-examined in any court of the United States, then according to the rules of the common law.

I will leave this one alone, for now at least. Perhaps as things progress, it might need some looking into but that's for later, if ever.

The Eighth Amendment

Excessive bail shall not be required, nor excessive fines imposed, nor cruel and unusual punishments inflicted.

Oh, we've gone far astray from this amendment, and have built a system which resembles more debtors prison than a justice system. It is not uncommon for someone to end up in jail only because they could not afford the excessive fines or come up with bail money and ended up sitting in prison for minor violations. This is a practice we will be ending, it is cruel in its application and causes excessive hardships upon the most vulnerable among us. No one should ever go to jail because they couldn't afford to pay a fine for something as minor as a seatbelt violation, and yet, all over our country this can, and does, happen. We will talk more about this in Legal Stuff.

The Ninth Amendment
The enumeration in the Constitution, of certain rights, shall not be construed to deny or disparage others retained by the people.

We, as a nation, need to embrace this amendment. Most do not even realize it exists and do not understand the power it could have on our society. When a law is brought up we will often talk about the First and the Second Amendment and how it applies, but rarely is this ever discussed when laws are being made to curtail the rights of individuals or groups, typically stemming from a religious belief, not a legal one. When we try to deny some of our citizens the rights enjoyed by the majority, this amendment should protect us, but it has been ignored in favor of granting more rights to some and less to others. But this amendment will play heavily into some of the changes we are going to be making when discussing *Nosy Neighbor Laws*.

The Tenth Amendment
The powers not delegated to the United States by the Constitution, nor prohibited by it to the States, are reserved to the States respectively, or to the people.

Essentially, this is the *get off my lawn* amendment. It gives the states the right to order its business, without interference from the federal government, provided it does not violate federal law. It's a dual-edged sword which has given rise to greatness, and plunged our nation into darkness, and we're just going to have to continue wrestling with it back and forth in all its glory and dismay as necessary.

So, that covers the first ten. We have more, some didn't work out so well, like prohibition, and others, like the abolishment of slavery, did. The Equal Rights Amendment, to this day, still hangs around in limbo just shy of the necessary states needed for it to become law. There will be more changes to come, and I hope by the end of this revolution of ours, you'll be proud of what we have accomplished while acknowledging there will always be more work to be done so we never slide back into the complacency that got us into this mess to begin with.

THE MEDIA

As your humble Dictator, I felt it prudent to address the media. In most dictatorships, media outlets are usually controlled and directed by the dictates of power, mere shadow puppets compared to what the media is capable of in free societies. During my reign, I wish to reassure the members of the media about my intentions. I expect the best you have to offer, if only so poor Walter Cronkite can stop spinning in his grave.

That being said, I expect the media to report the news with honesty and integrity and leave the spin to the PR people who are paid for such things. Our system has been overtaken by bias and gratuitous fear-mongering that has divided our country and even called into question the nature of reality, as our news stations broadcast spin instead of facts.

If a news station is broadcasting opinion, then it should be clearly understood it is an opinion being offered for public consumption, **not** facts. The blurring of the facts vs opinion needs to end, and our news should not be determined on ratings but in reality. Political leaning news stations must cease to call themselves news stations and be truthful with their audience about who, and what, they are. Stories are to be fact checked, and not abridged to give false impressions of reality to suit viewers personal biases.

During my reign, fake news outlets will come to an end, or overtly stamped "parody" or "opinion only" across all their broadcasts. The warping of our news has to end. And end it shall.

I will, in the beginning, allow stations to clean up their act on their own, but after six months, reviews will begin and if the spewing of misleading information continues, action will be taken. Beginning with fines and ending with the dismantling of entire news systems if I have to. I want honest news and genuine criticisms, but I will not tolerate the warping of reality anymore.

Other entertainment media outlets, please, continue to entertain. If I, your delightful Dictator, am the butt of those jokes, go for it. There will be no repercussions for creative expression.

I want people to have faith in our news, to know it is real and not question if it is honest. I want our news industry to flourish and inform our people of the important things happening in our neighborhoods, states, country, and the world. I want a free exchange of information from reporter to their listeners, without the seeds of doubt our current news media circus has brought us to. I want Walter Cronkite to be your patron saint and keep him as your guiding principle of integrity in the news, and strive to rebuild our news into something he would be proud to be a part of, rather than the shame it would bring him now.

A strong, independent, and free press is the backbone of any solid democracy. And we will need your strength in the coming years. It is upon your shoulders our country rests, so... don't fuck it up.

CIVIL FORFEITURES

As we briefly discussed earlier, civil forfeitures are something I plan on putting an end to in our country. But... well, I am Dictator, and I'm making one exception to this rule. Over the past decade, a small group of people have manipulated our system and brought our country to edge of collapse, all in the name of greed and personal power. I wish it to be known from this day forward, destructive greed will not be rewarded.

I have a list (don't we all have a list of people we'd like to bring to justice?) but suffice to say, if you have used your money and influence to undermine our country for your personal gain, I am coming for you. Your assets will be seized, your companies taken and turned into employee owned co-ops, and your freedoms ending in prison for crimes against our nation. Wealth will no longer insulate a person from the consequences of their actions. All will be held to the same code of conduct, and illicit activities no longer ignored simply because an individual was good at hoarding money.

There are problems to be solved in our country, many of them brought about by unmitigated greed, and we will use their money to start to put to right much of what has been wrong with our nation. This will not erase the atrocities done in the name of profit, but it will go a long way towards fixing them. Our country will need capital to correct the many problems we will be addressing in this book, and this is where we begin.

Still doing okay?

CHAPTER ONE
THE ENVIRONMENT

We're going to begin our revolution here, with the environment, because if you can't breathe, you can't live. It's really as simple as that. For far too long we have taken our world for granted, assuming no matter what indignities we heaped upon the earth, our world would somehow adjust and continue to support us. We now know that isn't true. Oh, the world can survive no matter what we do (outside of cracking our planet like an egg) but we, as a species, may not be able to survive what will come if we continue our wicked ways.

If we want to thrive, we are going to have to change. I understand, change is hard, and it can be scary, but that doesn't mean the reward isn't worth the risk. And, the risks we are taking by not changing are far too high for it not to be worth the reward of our efforts.

As you go through this book you're going to find the environment coming up in multiple places. Because the environment dictates almost every aspect of our lives, from where we live to how we live, the environment as much defines our existence as we define the world around us to meet our needs.

As much as I like lists and clearly defined categories, the fact remains, nothing resides inside a bubble unaffected by other bubbles. To quote Dirk Gently, it's all connected.

So, with that in mind, let's begin...

COOL IT DOWN

We're going to start with something simple (sigh of relief). The world is getting too hot, we know this, we also know the darker something is, the more heat it will absorb. It's why wearing black on a hot summer day isn't the best idea, unless you like sweating and panting of course, then I guess you do wear black on a hot summer day. But for the environment, sweating and panting isn't ideal.

So, to address this, I as your wonderful Dictator, hereby decree all highrise buildings do one of two things (look, I'm giving options here!) all flat roofs are either to be painted with white reflective paint OR turn those empty spaces into green growing areas. Build containers and plant grasses, fruits, vegetables, roses, whatever makes your heart sing, and go for it. Turn your rooftop into a small piece of paradise on earth were you and the residents of your building can go and enjoy a bit of green in their own backyard, so to speak.

Or, you can be lazy and just paint it white. Also, a perfectly acceptable option, if not so pretty or enjoyable. The point is, in areas that have started this, the average temperatures has gone down as more heat is being reflected back up rather than pulled down. And we need to start somewhere, and this seems like the place to start.

Later on, we are going to talk about solar roofing and roads, green tech, and community gardens as an integrated part of helping ourselves and our environment, so if you want to flip ahead to those chapters, that's fine, I'll wait here for you to return. Otherwise, let's talk about some other things we can do.

In an effort to cool down our cities, we are going to start incorporating trees and plants into our city planning. In new areas of construction, all sidewalk areas will have a green strip, equal to the width of the sidewalk, between the sidewalk and the road with a mix of grasses, plants, flowers, and trees as part of the design.

For places already established, planter gardens will be added at regular intervals. They will rotate through a mix of fruiting plants and trees, flowers, and grasses. We will start this project at the city centers and move our way out. The plants and trees chosen will have the secondary effect of free food for the picking for the local community.

Super Trees are also a valid option for our city centers. These are vertical growing structures that capture rainwater, filter exhaust, and have solar panels at the top to help light the city at night. Not only are they efficient at bringing down city temperatures, improving air quality, and lower lighting costs, they are ascetically pleasing as well.

But, who's going to maintain all this new green stuff, you ask. We'll get more into this in *The Economy* under *A Year of Giving*. Don't worry, I have a plan.

They are doing amazing things all over the world to bring down carbon immersions, improve air quality, and making our world just a little bit better with each project. I want our country to become a leader in this, but first, we have to learn from others who have already taken those first steps. My goal is to make each city in our country as self-sustaining as possible.

As part of this overall plan, new standards will be made to address global warming and self-sustaining infrastructure throughout our country. All new construction will meet, or exceed, the new regulations we will create to bring this new technology into every aspect of our lives. We are not looking for one solution to all of our problems, there isn't one. Instead, we will use what we have and build on it to find other, and better, solutions as we go. We will also be joining the rest of the world and sign the Paris Accord.

We have lived far too long taking our world for granted. The world can go on without us, but we cannot go on without the world to sustain us. There is no exit plan if we ruin our world, there is no Plan B. It will be up to each and every one of us to do all that we can to bring our way of living more in harmony with the needs of the planet.

Our state and national parks are the gems of our nation and should be treated, and protected, as such. Due to industrial expansion and urban sprawl, these practices have begun encroaching on our national lands in the name of progress. It ends. Now.

As your humble Dictator, I do so decree that no new construction or development, of any kind, shall take place within one mile of the border of any state or national park. Existing housing can be left, but no new construction of any kind will be permitted.

Since it is my hope with the expansion of green tech, the old industries of gas, oil, and coal extraction will soon end, no new contracts will be allowed in those industries going forward. What you have, is what you have. Any pending contracts or tracks of land that have not been developed but are held by those industries will be forfeited back to the state to be added to nature restoration projects in those states. In addition to no new expansion, any area devastated by the extraction process, those companies will be required to clean up and restore those tracks of land back to its natural state as they scale down operations. Companies will clean up the mess they've made.

I want you, my faithful followers, to be able to enjoy the natural wonders of our country.

Now, you may have noticed I mentioned nature restoration projects a little bit ago and may be wondering what I am talking about. These areas will not officially be a part of our state or national parks, but left to grow wild after a reintroduction of native plants. They will not be mowed or maintained, they will simply be allowed to grow and flourish as nature intended.

If such a track of land is adjacent to a public park and wishes to annex it for park use, that will be allowed. But no private developer will be allowed to encroach upon those areas without first providing evidence, on both a state and federal level, expansion would be for the common good of the people living in that area, with 80% of the benefits going to the local population.

If, at some point in the future, it was deemed necessary for road expansion to go through a protected parcel of land, it will be done with as little disturbance to the natural state of the land, and animal crossing bridges will be an integrated part of the construction process.

We need to stop thinking the world will just somehow absorb our trash and continue on uninterrupted. We need to protect and cherish the natural beauty of the world and work hard to keep our home from becoming one big landfill. We'll talk more about this in later chapters, but for now, let's clean up our act, and our mess, before it's too late.

PIPELINES

Okay, can we all agree that oil and gas pipelines are bad? Good! We know they are, no matter how many times some company tells us they're safe, we can see evidence to the contrary wherever we look. Leaks, explosions, water sources contaminated, local wildlife and human health devastated by their mere presence roll across our newsfeeds almost daily.

Now, when it comes to these pipelines, the majority of what is being transported does not go to powering our country. Most of it is sent to coastal cities to be refined and shipped elsewhere in the world. The pipelines only benefit the corporations who profit from them. We pay for it, and they profit from it.

Under *Energy*, I will be talking more about green tech and expanding our national energy grid to include individual houses and buildings as part of the grid, which will more than make up for any minor losses we may have from shutting down the pipelines. We are going to move away from a centralized grid to a decentralized one that doesn't depend on any one area for operations. As it stands, those pipelines are damaging our country, and our people, and do almost nothing except add to our problems.

So, henceforth, I command, as your delightful Dictator, no new pipelines will be permitted in our country.

But still, that leaves all the ones already here to deal with. They need to be removed, but safely. To be truthful, I don't have enough expertise in pipeline construction to give you a decent plan for their removal. But, I do know there are people out there with the necessary knowledge, and I will be counting on you to help me come up with a plan to fix this situation.

Because I know it isn't just a matter of pulling up the pipes and throwing them away. It would be nice if the solution was as simple as that, but unfortunately, it is not.

What I do know is, as each section of pipe is removed, wildlife restoration will need to be integrated into the process, as well as cleaning up contaminated water systems. And we'll need to figure out what to do with all the leftover piping. Seriously, what do we do with it? Just throwing the pipes away in a landfill is not what I would consider a reasonable option, for a variety of reasons, so the question is, what is a good idea? Anyone with a good idea, please step forward, I'm looking forward to hearing from you.

A WORLD OF GREEN

Every year we cut down around 4 billion trees to sustain nothing but the paper industries worldwide. That's a lot of trees. Trees can take up to 20 years to mature enough to be harvested and we are currently cutting down trees faster than they can be replenished. And the simple fact is, we don't need to.

Let's take a few minutes to sing the praises of hemp.

Okay, calm down everyone. First of all, I'm talking about hemp here, not marijuana, they are two entirely different plants and hemp may be one of the most useful plants to grow on earth. (I will, by the way, under *Legal Stuff*, be talking about marijuana, but it's not relevant to our discussion here.)

One acre of hemp can replace 4 acres of trees for harvesting. A tree takes 20 years to grow, hemp 90 days to full maturity, which means, depending on the area, 2 - 4 rotations could be planted every year. It needs little care and no pesticides. It can be planted almost anywhere and in places traditional crops can't be grown, expanding available land for farmers. It is hardy, easy to grow, requires less water than traditional crops, and versatile in its uses.

Not only can hemp be used to replace all paper manufacturing in the U.S. (with fewer chemicals and less stink) but it can be used as fiber for clothing, canvas, and rope. But, the wonders of hemp doesn't end there. It can be used to make fiberglass, plastics, heating oil, soaps, paints, insulation, particleboard, fiberboard, stable bedding, inks, oils and even diesel fuel, and the list goes on. There are over 29,000 uses for hemp in our daily lives, meaning it can be used in everything from medicine to how we build our homes, all while being low impact on our environment.

In saving our environment, hemp is one of the first small steps that will reap big rewards.

So, with that in mind, I hereby decree as your faithful Dictator, hemp is now legal, everywhere. And taking a page from our Founding Father's, require every farmer to utilize a minimum of 10% of their farmland for hemp. Within the first year of my dictatorship, all paper producers are to switch over from tree pulp to hemp for all paper production. Within the second year, plastic manufacturers are to switch over from petroleum based plastics to hemp based ones.

By the end of my term as your dictator, I want to see a full scale implementation of hemp in every aspect of our lives as fully and practically as possible.

Now, as to what all of those will be will in large part be up to you. Stop looking around, yes, I mean you. Those choices are going to be largely made on what we buy, so if you, as consumers, start showing a progressive preference for hemp based products, the manufactures will respond in kind. Some industries will be forced over, like paper mills, but others like clothing manufacturers, are going to be voluntary (at least, unless some experts can show me why it would be in the best interest of the environment to force the change) so make your purchases count people.

It's up to us to fix the mess we've made of the planet. We're in this together, so let's do our best, shall we?

RECYCLING

Years ago our country started recycling, but it's rather haphazard, largely depending on how much cash a city can get for what it collects and ignores what doesn't show a profit. Well, I hate to break the bad news to you, but not all of our decisions can be made on profit margins, sometimes it's just going to have to be about doing the right thing.

The amount of trash we are generating can't be sustained, particularly since much of what we make will take multiple lifetimes to degrade, if ever. Our trash floats in the oceans and stretches across our land, it's everywhere, even places humans never go deal with our leftovers.

And this can't just be about recycling our personal garbage, but containing our far flung debris all over the world. Then our next problem is, once we retrieve it, we have to figure out what to do with it. Dumping all of it in landfills doesn't really solve the problem, so we're going to have to do better. I'm sure you've heard the phrase, "reduce, reuse, recycle" and it's a good start, but we need to step it up to the next level.

Anything that can be recycled, will be. Food waste will be turned into community compost, along with the rest of our lawn leavings. Petroleum based plastics and non-biodegradable containers will be replaced by other more eco-friendly options. Every day, in every way, we must begin to become more conscientious about our trash habits and work together to reduce what gets thrown uselessly away.

Our personal habits are making a mess of our world, but our industrial waste is devastating our planet. From supermarkets to superconductors, we need to reduce the amount of leftover ick currently tolerated as an acceptable part of doing business. And here, yet again, I, as your concerned Dictator, will ask for your help. I will need experts to come forward and help create a plan to change how we deal with our trash, and find ways to cope with what we've already made. Everything from turning it into sustainable housing to eliminating a product or manufacturing technique that is inherently wasteful.

So, step up people and be a part of the solution. Each of us in our own way can make a difference, and together we can make a huge impact on how we deal with our leftovers.

FEMA

While talking about the Environment we need to touch briefly on FEMA before we move on. Considering all the natural disasters that have hit our country over the past few years (and escalating) I'm sure most of you are at least familiar with this agency. If not, FEMA stands for Federal Emergency Management Agency, your to-go in case of emergency in our country, forest fire, earthquake, tornado, hurricane, mudslide, volcanic eruption, they cover it all. If some act of nature has knocked over your community, they step in and help dig you out and, in theory, give you funds to help rebuild and get your life back in order.

This agency has often been neglected, underfunded and not always headed by someone who actually knows how to manage a disaster. In our current state of global climate change and all the damage caused by the weather changes it brings, we need to take this agency very seriously and bolster its funding and, possibly, even expand its directives, for all our safety.

So, from here on out, no one can be placed in charge of this (or honestly ***any***) agency without the proper education and experience needed to effectively manage that department. Appointments to any agency should be based on merit, not political pull.

Second, funding for FEMA needs to be increased to deal with the ever expanding threat of natural disasters affecting our communities. Because sometimes, and this is one of those times, throwing money at a situation is the correct solution.

We have many challenges ahead of us, and dealing with climate change is going to be one of them. We need to start rethinking how we will rebuild communities who have suffered from extreme weather, and perhaps, even giving back to nature some of the land we have excessively modified for our use. Relocation is never easy, but it may be the best solution, and if it is, those displaced will be compensated for their losses and given assistance in settling into a new life somewhere else.

With new advances come new and better ways to build housing, roads, and infrastructure, it is now time to implement those advances. Let us go boldly forward to meet the challenges that await us with confidence, knowing we are a capable species with the courage to face and overcome whatever happens. I have faith in us, I hope you do too.

If you need to a moment to process, I understand.

CHAPTER TWO
THE ECONOMY

I'm going to let you in on a little secret... money isn't real. I'm being serious here, it really isn't. Money is nothing more than an agreed upon fiction for simplifying transactions between consumers and producers. Our money is based on nothing, there used to be a gold standard, where every dollar could be exchanged for the equivalent in gold or other predetermined tangible items. But those days are no longer and our money is now just an accounting system held up by our hopes, dreams, and collective agreement to honor it.

And, while we're talking about shattering illusions, let's take a few minutes to talk about the free market you hear so much about in capitalism. It's not real either. At least, it only exists as far as we humans define it. It does not have an independent life outside of the rules and regulations we give it. The market will not "correct itself" any more than broken computer code can without our active help. Capitalism, the market, money, all of these things are artificial constructs we have made for ourselves to regulate the sale of goods. And, we can change the rules any time we want to. We can strengthen the markets through regulation to make them more equal or we can let them spiral out of control like a cascade failure on a computer, it is entirely up to us. All of it is a pretend game we made the rules for and we have all, more or less, agreed to treat as real.

Even our money is mostly pretend, considering only 8% of the world's money is actually physical. All the rest is held in electronic accounts spread out around the world and held by various banks and institutions. In a way, our world's banking system is run like a credit card. Every time we go to the bank and ask for money, if we are approved, we are given either a check and we deposit in our account, or we may never see it as a computer sends an amount to another institution to cover a debt we owe.

But, you see, the bank didn't genuinely have that money on hand, there's no secret vault to keep all their lending money in. It's all pretend, a made up I.O.U. from the bank, issued to us. And then we pay them back with another set of I.O.U.'s called cash. But then again, in this day and age, we may not ever physically touch so much as a single dollar bill, as our employers' direct deposit our paychecks and we use debit cards, checks, and electronic transfers to move money around. It's just bits of 0's and 1's rolling around a computer system telling us it's real.

Governments do the same thing. Aside from the small amount of currency they create in paper money and coins, the rest is computer generated. Our government gives out I.O.U.'s the same as the banks do, and then we pay into those generated debts with taxes, which again is just another form of I.O.U. going back the other way.

It's all pretend.

Now that's not to say poverty or wealth isn't real. But it **is** an artificially created system. Nor am I saying money isn't useful. It is. Because it's a lot easier to hand someone a dollar bill than carry around a chicken to exchange if you need something. But we need to start realizing money isn't anything more than a useful tool, not an intrinsic item of wealth. And when we hear the words, "*But where will the money come from?!*" Remember this, money is only as real as we imagine it to be, no more, no less.

Now that I've shattered your illusions of what money is, let's go on to banking.

BANKING

While you're still internally debating on if money is real or not, let's talk about banks. There was a time in our not too distant past when we had two types of banks, one was for boring banking. You know, checking and savings accounts, home loans, and small personal loans, maybe a few small business loans would come through every now and again, but that was about it. It was boring and it was, for the most part, safe.

The banks would issue loans, and charge interest on them to cover their expenses and keep the doors open. They issued credit only after careful consideration to make sure if someone couldn't pay them back it wouldn't take down every other person banking with them or the bank itself. And each bank had enough reserves to survive someone not paying them back nor acquired any debt they couldn't cover with their own reserves.

The other kind of bank was speculative banking. Where an institution or a bank takes our money and uses it to make more money through investments, the Stock Market, or other acquisitions with the idea those investments will pay back more than they spent getting them. This is called high risk banking, you are betting you can make more money from the money you already have. Sometimes it works out, but as any gambler could tell you, sometimes it doesn't. And when it doesn't, it's a bad day for someone, probably a lot of someones.

And in the past, these two types of banking were kept separate from each other. It allowed people to keep their money safe in a stable, generally non-risk bank, and could choose if they wanted to, to go to another bank if they had money they'd like to risk on betting correctly. They could choose to jump in with entire groups doing the same called Investment firms or stockbrokers, and pool their resources for what they hoped would be an even bigger payout when they finished playing, like IRA's.

But over the years, the walls separating those two types of banking were broken down, and even boring banks began to risk your money, often without consulting their clients about their actions. And the risk side kept increasing, banks handed out more and more I.O.U.'s they knew they could never cover if things went bad, and still continued because, oh... the possible rewards of avarice blinded them to the reality of the consequences if they choose poorly.

And starting in 2007 their house of cards fell down, taking huge swathes of the rest of us with them. People who had never gambled in their lives, saved their money and always paid their bills, were suddenly wiped out. Homes and retirement savings were lost seemly overnight. Lives were ruined. People were unexpectedly bankrupt through no fault of their own.

And the banks *tsked, tsked* and demanded we give them more money to clean up the mess they made so they could save themselves. Not their customers, not the people who had put their faith in them when they placed their money with them, no... those people were on their own. Sorry folks, not our problem, even if it was our fault.

And sadly, that's exactly what our old government did. So, the banks survived the crisis they had generated with their greed, and the people suffered and paid for it. A few new laws were passed and the banks screamed and so a few of those bills went away almost as fast as they had come into existence. And banks went back, more or less, to what they had been doing before the collapse, with a shrug to our concerns because they still didn't think it was their problem. And after the way the government rushed in to bail them out, and let them keep the money they had taken from us, they had no reason to think otherwise. To them, it was all reward, no risk, because they believed the government would always bail them out and they would never have to pay the price for their failures. Everything could always go on, business as usual, and either way, they'd still able to rake in as much money (and about 10% more) than the traffic could bear, whatever the actual outcome.

Yeah. That's gotta stop. Don't you agree?

So, you may now be asking, what *are* we going to do about it? Simple. First, we go back to the two banking systems. Each type of bank will clearly indicate what kind of bank it is. If someone wants to risk their money for a possible reward, then that's their choice. But, and to be clear on this, it **is** their choice, and they may not wish to gamble so they may choose a nice, boring bank and live happily knowing the bank cannot risk their money. It is, and will remain, mostly, safe.

Now, on to the more exciting part of banking, with all their risks and possible rewards. If you want to engage in this type of investing, go for it. BUT, you're on your own. There will be no F.D.I.C. insurance for your gambling. If you bring down your entire bank, well, then your bank will be parted out and sold to cover your debts. And your assets will now always exceed your investments by a minimum of 10%. There will be yearly audits conducted, by a competitor, just to keep you all honest. Each bank auditor will be randomly assigned each year to review all listed assets and overall investments, if at any time the balance shifts toward debt over assets, you'd better be ready to start selling something off to make it balance again. You can gamble, but you are no longer allowed to be reckless.

Now, there will be a third type of bank opened as well. It has been a proposal over the years, and I agree the idea is a good one. For many in low income areas, there are no banks, of any kind, in their neighborhood. These are places where check cashing services are their only option and they pay dearly for it. So, going forward, every post office will also add banking to their list of services. Nice, boring banking. You can open a checking and savings account, get small, personal loans with reasonable interest rates, and save for retirement at any post office.

No matter what city you are in, if you go to a post office, you can access your account, withdraw or deposit money or pay your bills. To help with that, each bank will have dedicated, secured computers for their customers to manage their money and pay their bills if they do not have access to a computer in their home.

Now that I've mentioned check cashing services, let's talk about them for a bit, shall we? Your freewheeling days of charging to cash checks and outrageous payday loan interest rates are a thing of the past. You have been legal loan sharks for far too long and it will end, now. You will no longer be able to line your pockets on the backs of the poor by offering them loans you know they will never be able to pay back in any reasonable amount of time.

And to that end, effective immediately, your loan rates will no longer be whatever you decide they are (400% or more APR? I mean, seriously, come on!), instead, they cannot exceed federal loan rates. If you're going to pretend to be a bank, you're going to be governed by the same laws as a bank. All current loans you have out, their rates will drop to fall in line with federal standards for banks. If you attempt to circumvent this, any loan that doesn't comply will be forgiven and you'll just have to suck up the loss. If you go bankrupt, then I would suggest you learn a new trade or get better at this one and try again at a later time. If you can get anyone to loan you the money to start again.

Oh, credit cards. A blessing and the curse of modern money. They can be a lifesaver in case of emergency, and a life ender if squandered. You've made a great deal of money by playing fast and loose and charging excessive rates for interest. You've given out credit to those you knew couldn't pay and handed out credit limits far exceeding what you knew someone could afford.

I will acknowledge you are a necessary evil, but it doesn't make you good. So, we need some new rules governing your practices. To begin with, you cannot extend credit beyond 5% of a person's yearly salary. And no person shall be able to carry more than 20% of their salary total in credit. So, if a person makes $20,000 a year, a single credit card company could not issue a credit limit above $1000, nor exceed $4000 in total credit card extension from multiple companies.

Nor can any credit card charge more than 5 points higher than federal interest rates. You can extend credit, but you are not going to be allowed to gouge people for the convenience of going into debt with you.

Okay, I think that covers the basics of banking, for now. But I will admit I am not a banking expert, and so I will be relying on those experts for help in hammering out the finer details of this current mess. I'm open to suggestions to make this vital area of our country better, more accessible, reasonable and stable.

And with that thought, let's take a few minutes to address poverty...

ADDRESSING POVERTY

Poverty is at the heart of fixing the economy. It can seem so overwhelming, when it's everywhere and nothing seems to make it go away, no matter what we do about it. But, there are things we can do about, we just need to change how we look at poverty and our approach to solving the poverty problem. You know, change everything.

Right now, our wages rise so slowly in comparison to inflation, by the time we receive a raise, adjusted for inflation, we're pretty much back to what we were making before the raise in terms of spending power. We're on a treadmill, pulling in all our effort, but never going anywhere.

We spend so much of our time working to make ends meet, even if we have a little extra left over, we're so tired and overworked we can't enjoy spending what we've earned. We are trading our lives an hour at a time, and the return we are getting for our investment is nowhere near compensation for what we have lost, in most cases. And for the economy to run, we need people to spend money. How else are all those things we make going to get sold to justify a company making them to begin with?

Now, I'm going to tell you something you may not believe, but in truth, we don't need to work 40 hours a week to power our system. Our productivity is the highest it's ever been in history. We can make more stuff, in less time, with less effort than ever before. Unfortunately, that has not been reflected in our wages or in the number of hours we're required to work to be considered "full-time".

We're still wedded to the idea that only through long, life-breaking hours can we justify our getting ahead. It's been drilled into us for our entire lives, if you do everything right, make no mistakes, study hard, work hard, give your all to your employer, give up birthdays and holidays when asked, take no (or few) vacations, and dedicate yourself to the pursuit of money, you will be rewarded for all your sacrifices. Except, it doesn't work that way for most of us, does it?

We follow the directive given to us, thinking we are going to make it, and then the company you work for closes, to only reopen in another country. Or the CEO demands you exchange part of your wages or retirement or benefits if you want the company to stay, leaving you employed but desperate. Or they cut your hours and hire more part-time or temp workers to fill the gap. Few companies have loyalty to their workers, only seeing them as part of their bottom line, not a person. The American Dream of getting ahead drifts further away with every step we take, all in the name of profit and an outdated idea of hard work always equals success.

So, here we go, I have six years to address this problem, so let's get to it.

WAGES

Wages should be a recognition of the time we are trading for a paycheck. So, with that in mind, I hereby declare as your humble leader the following...

Year One, (you'll be able to hear the corporations screams from space, but that's okay, they'll get over it) everyone gets a living wage. Within the first six months, the new minimum wage is going to be raised to a living wage. If you work full time, you should earn enough to live on. It's fair. You are giving your life an hour at a time in exchange for money, so you should be able to have a life outside of work as part of your investment.

After a bit of time, businesses start to experience an uptick in demand for their products/services. People are going out a bit more, buying items they've desperately needed but put off because they couldn't afford them. Restaurants start seeing a gain in customers with a little extra cash to spend. The economy starts to roll along a little more smoothly for everyone without the constant panic of "*Can I afford to live this week?*" dominating our thoughts and overriding our purchases.

Year Three, (hear those screams, they'll be loud but they're gonna be okay) official full-time is now 30 hours a week, and minimum wage is raised correspondingly. Oh my, you now have enough money to live on AND a bit more time to spend it. How about that? Ten more hours a week you can spend with family, go out to eat, watch a movie and not have to scramble quite so hard to scratch out some time to do it. You're feeling a little more rested and relaxed, and you're giving the economy a boost with your newly acquired free time.

Businesses start to notice another uptick in demand. People have more free time to spend their money and are going out more, spending more, doing more things and going more places, and that all adds up to more demand. Businesses profit margins begin to grow, and while productivity is now meeting demand, there's more incentive to think about adding a few more employees on. The grumbles subside a little bit in the wake of more profits.

Year Five, (they're going to scream again, but we've gotten used to it by now and have learned to ignore it like we do when children have a temper tantrum) full-time is now 20 hours a week, minimum wage raises correspondingly. Oh my god, what are we going to do with our time?! You mean I have the time to read a book or enjoy a coffee at a cafe and stare out into space and not feel bad for wasting the precious time I used to have so little of?

You mean I can get more sleep and not be exhausted all the time trying to fit in everything into the day until I fell down from exhaustion? I have time, I have money, I have a life, and I feel good most of the time now. I don't get sick as much or call in when there's nothing wrong just because I'm exhausted and need a break. My productivity goes up at work because I'm not feeling pulled in 20 different directions or overwhelmed with thoughts of desperation, wondering if I'll make it through the week.

Businesses now pay heed to demand exceeding productivity and have no choice but to hire more workers if they're going to keep up. Profits are at an all-time high as people spend their time in pursuit of happiness and they're spending more money as they do. Unemployment plummets and workers have more power because they are now in demand, those slots have to be filled if the company is going to keep up with their customer's spending. CEO's are too busy trying to met supply demands to do more than occasionally grumble under their breath about the good ole days when all of that profit would have gone to them, but not often or loudly, they want to be seen as a good place to work if they're going to attract employees to work for them who now have their pick of places.

Year Six. Things are going pretty good for everyone, poverty is the lowest it's ever been. The population is generally happier, healthier and more fit. People are more secure, and crime is now at an all-time low without the economic pressure of poverty driving it. Domestic violence figures start to go down as stress levels and feelings of inadequacy begin to diminish. Alcoholism and drug abuse rates continue to fall as people no longer feel the need to drown themselves in an altered state to cope with a bleak existence. Xenophobia begins to fade as people have more time to travel and experience new cultures and see that everywhere they go, people are people, just like them.

Life is worth living for the majority of Americans now as they shake their heads at the bad ole days of low wages and fear. Life is good and getting better.

AWAY FROM THE GRIND

We all need downtime. We are not machines, we all need a break every now and again to sleep in, be lazy, do nothing and not feel any lingering guilt. Study after study has shown vacations are not only good for us, but beneficial to our employers. When we take regular breaks from work, we return more focused, more productive, and generally better at our jobs.

So, with that in mind, I hereby declare...

Vacations

Every employee is to be given 30 days of paid vacation a year, to be taken all at once or spaced out throughout the year. Nor can an employer offer extra cash in exchange for not taking vacation time. We all need vacation time, and you're going to take it whether you want to or not. Hibernate like a bear during your vacation if you don't want to do anything, but you're gonna use your vacation time.

But since you're going to collect the time, I would suggest you take your vacation time to see a bit of the world or try a new hobby or go to your favorite cafe and let the coffee cups pile up while you watch the world move around you. Take some time to relax, breath, reassess your life, take a nap, and do something that makes you happy. Life is short, enjoy it.

Family Leave

Family is important, whether you're bringing a child into this world or being there for a close family member at the end of theirs. There are moments in our lives when family has to come before work, and Family Leave is the way to recognize their importance.

Now, there are no hard and fast rules for family emergencies, but guidelines can be put in place to cover most situations.

A death in the family can be tragic. A lingering death, even harder. It takes time to recover from something so life altering, and is especially important at the beginning. If you have lost someone important in your life or watching over someone during their last days, paid time off should be given for up to a month. If you need more time, you can use whatever you have remaining of your vacation time, to have up to two months of full paid leave. If there are extenuating circumstance, an additional month can be granted, at half pay, and an additional 2 months given unpaid without fear of losing your job.

Tragedy can strike in many forms, a heart attack, cancer, compound injuries from an accident can happen at any time, often without warning. If something like this happens to a family member (or to you), you should be able to take time off to care for them. General guidelines for injuries or health conditions are as follows, up to a month of full paid leave initially. An additional 4 months can be granted at half pay in cases of lingering illnesses such as cancer or severe injuries. An additional 6 months at no pay can be given without fear of job loss, and they can use their 30 days of paid vacation if they have it available at any time during this, giving an employee up to a year to deal with a catastrophic family emergency.

The birth of a child is a special moment, it is a time for bonding and learning about the new life you have brought into this world. It's also a time for recovery for the mother, and a time for your significant other to bond with the newest member of the family. The time leading up to birth is also important, and sometimes complications can arise that requires a mother to be put on bedrest for the sake of their health.

With that in mind, here are the guidelines for pregnancy and maternal/partner leave. If a woman is put on bed rest or ordered by a doctor not to work at any point during her pregnancy, she is immediately granted paid leave that continues until 2 months after the birth. If a mother chooses to stay home with her child after that, she can take an additional 10 months off at half pay without fear of losing her job. Partner leave, prior to the birth, if your significant other needs care, you can use your family leave. After the birth of the child, you can take up to 30 days paid leave to stay at home and bond with your child and can take an additional month off at half pay. You can also take an additional 10 months off with no pay without fear of losing your job.

For adoptive parents. The primary caregiver is given two months off at full pay, and an additional 10 months of half-pay. The non-primary parent is allowed one month of paid family leave, and an additional month of leave at half pay, and up to an additional 10 months off with no pay without fear of losing your job.

Sick Time

We all get sick, it happens and there's nothing we can do about it. On the other hand, being forced to go to work while sick is something we can do something about. If you are sick, stay home! There's no reason to make everyone else around you sick and keep spreading your germs around.

With that in mind, every employee gets 12 paid sick days a year, and can be used up to 3 consecutive days at a time. If an employee goes over 12 days for the year, or three days consecutively and needs more time, they'll need to get a note from a doctor excusing them from work to be paid. If your illness goes over 15 consecutive days, then the employee is switched over from sick time to family leave time for the duration.

I think that pretty much covers most situations. Again, life can be surprising and it's the only thing stranger than fiction, so some flexibility needs to be built into the system. But, however you slice it, it's better than the system we currently have and we can always work towards a better system as needed. Life has to be about more than work, and work should never be more important than the life you are given. Life will go on without you, no one is irreplaceable when it comes to a job, but to your family and friends, you can never be replaced. Our laws and our society need to change to recognize the basic idea of how precious life really is and not demand we squander the whole of our existence on work.

A YEAR OF GIVING

I'm sure everyone reading this is familiar with the Peace Corps. If not, here's a quick overview, people volunteer to spend a set amount of time helping others, usually in underprivileged areas around the world. Some of you are also probably aware of the U.S. equivalent program, AmeriCorps and does basically the same thing, but in our country.

Under my rule, the AmeriCorps program is about to be expanded, to include every young person after graduation for one year. Waivers can be given for disabilities that prohibit a person from living independently or if an individual wishes to join the military or the Peace Corps instead. But, outside of that, every graduating high school student, rich, poor, or anything in between will be required to give a year of service to their country, outside of their normal community.

It will be part job training, part community service. At the beginning of their senior year, each student will be required to fill out an information sheet that will include things such as career aspirations, hobbies, interests, and abilities. At the end of their senior year, they will be sent information regarding their assignment for the year.

Each young adult will be assigned to a city where they will spend the next year helping to improve their new community. Community housing, food, and a small stipend will be provided for each person. During this time, they will not be allowed to accept any supplemental income from any outside source, each person will be treated exactly the same and given the exact same living accommodations. Each person will be allowed to take as much of their personal belongings they can fit into one backpack and one suitcase, but cannot exceed what they can carry on their own. (Certain exceptions can be made to accommodate disabilities) Choose wisely, because this is what you are going to have for your year away from home.

Some of the jobs (but not limited to) to be performed by the AmeriCorps will be helping out in underserved hospitals, clinics, nursing homes, long term care facilities, or helping the elderly or those needing assistance care who live at home. Or assigned to civic restoration projects, such as maintaining parks, the green tree street projects, keeping streets and sidewalks clean, painting murals, or community gardens. Or assigned to community daycares, child development programs, youth sports programs, arts and music programs, or other youth enrichment programs. Or assigned to housing projects, building projects, or urban development programs.

Okay, I think you get the idea. For one year, each person will help out their assigned community to make it better in some way, with the idea of matching career aspirations with the program they are assigned to.

Much of what is wrong with our country comes from a feeling of disconnection from each other outside of the community we have grown up in. Privilege has insulated the rich from the realities of life for the average person, and the poor often never experience life outside of 50 miles from where they were born. Our country has a million jobs needing to be filled but lack of funding has kept them from being done. This program addresses those problems with a practical solution that benefits everyone.

AmeriCorps will also allow anyone up to age 25 to volunteer to join if they are over 18. And, anyone within the program can opt to stay in for up to 5 years if they want to continue helping other communities. Those who volunteer for 5 years and wish to remain indefinitely as part of the program can opt to become employed as community supervisors or planners for AmeriCorps.

If you are wondering where the money for this program will come from, I will be redirecting a portion of the previous military budget for this program. We spend more money on our military than the next 10 countries down the line, often to the detriment of everything else. Before any of you come unglued at the idea of reassigning money previously earmarked for the military, I have a question for you. What are we protecting if there's nothing worth protecting at home? I will be addressing this more fully under *The Military*, but for now, just accept my assertion, the military budget can afford this.

UNIVERSAL BASIC INCOME

Okay, something tells me you were all with me up until you read Universal Basic Income. Some of you may not know what it is, while others may be screaming capitalism and calling for my removal as your faithful dictator.

For those who don't know what UBI is, here's the long and the short of it. Every adult, regardless of age, occupation, or income receives a monthly basic living allowance from the government, with no strings attached. If you are a billionaire, you receive the same amount as someone who makes zero a year. It's the exact same amount and doesn't go up or down in relation to income, automatically start on your 18th birthday and ends with your death. That's what Universal Basic Income is, ensuring every citizen receives a basic living allowance for their entire adult life.

But how will we pay for something like that??? Is your next question I'm sure. The answer is, in several different ways, part of the funding will come from our taxes, but the rest, well, let's just get right to it and begin.

We currently have a patchwork of programs to help those in need, often with gaps you could drive a truck through that people fall between all the time. The list of eligibility changes from program to program, state to state, and even Congress to Congress, leaving behind a trail of broken lives in its wake. There's no unifying theme to any of it, so let's fix that.

First on the list is the elimination of all other social support programs and consolidating all of them into Universal Basic Income. Social Security, Disability, unemployment, Aide to Dependent Families, Food Stamps, workman's comp, okay you get the idea... they are now all rolled into one single program. No more paperwork, no more having to prove you are worthy, no more jumping through hoops as you wait to find out your fate, it's just there, month after month, steady and reliable.

All those offices, all the paperwork, all that effort, all the money wasted trying to prove or disprove eligibility, *poof*, gone. No more lawyers needed to file paperwork, or judges needed to determine eligibility, no more doctor's notes and reams of paperwork to prove need. No more caseworkers, investigation agencies, no more court cases about possible fraud cluttering up our system or sapping resources from helping people.

You simply file your social security number with the IRS before you turn 18 and voila, you're done.

Onward to funding...

You may be unaware of this, but did you know over 70% of all innovations and around 90% of all new drug discoveries are paid for by your tax dollars? Through our taxes, the government pays colleges, universities, think tanks, and research sites to, well... research stuff. Some projects come to absolutely nothing, but a good chunk does come to something, in the form of new drugs, tech, gadgets and gizmos that once their worth is verified, are bought up by big corporations, patented and sold back to us for a profit. Basically, we pay for it, they profit from it, all at our expense.

All those commercials you've seen for some big corporation showing labs and people with beakers doing sciencey stuff? Yeah, those are mostly PR lies. They don't do the research, they just buy it, and tweak it for commercial use. Millions of tax dollars are spent every year for these companies to profits billions from our investment. Doesn't seem fair, does it? Yeah, me either.

So, as your delightful dictator, I hereby make the following proclamation...

From this moment forward, if a project was paid for with government funds, the research can no longer be sold outright, instead, the government will lease it to the most qualified bidder for the term of twenty years, after which, the bid goes back up for sale. With their lease, the company will pay the owners, i.e. the American people 10% of their sales for as long as they hold the patent.

As a nation, we will begin investing even more money into research programs. We have seen the wonders research has brought us, from the internet to Velcro to helping map the human genome. In recent years, federal funding for public research has fallen, and the innovations our country was once known for has dropped off correspondingly. Even with all the data showing public funding of research pays back manifold what we put into it, the quest for ever smaller budgets and austerity has had a detrimental effect on all research, both public and private, since the private sector is reliant on public research to build upon.

So, we will fund these programs and encourage new lines of thought and new ways of doing things, and we will once again begin reaping the rewards of research. And this time, every citizen will benefit from it with all the money generated from leasing these new wonders will go to funding the Universal Basic Income. We, as taxpayers, have paid for this research and we should be entitled to the profits from our investment.

For the rest, you can read more ideas on how to fund this in the next chapter, *Taxes*.

But before you move on, let's talk about why we should do this. First, because it's the right thing to do. As a nation, we have a responsibility to care for one another. When someone falls, we aren't supposed to walk over them, we are supposed to help them back up. That, more than anything, defines a society. Not how we help those with the most, but those with the least.

If we didn't need one another, there would be no reason to form tribes, much less cities or nations. We would be loners, making it all on our own with little to no contact with other human beings except to mate. But that's not how we live, we are social creatures, and we band together because we know we are stronger together than we are individually.

Now, let's talk about what UBI can do for you, personally, and why you want this in your life. Have you ever wanted to take a year off to write a book? Did you have an amazing idea for something and just needed some time to figure out how to make it work? Did you want to start your own business but were afraid to take the risk because you can't afford to leave your job? Are you an artist, musician, poet, painter, maker of creations, but you can't dedicate yourself to your craft because you like eating too much to quit your job? Did you want to go to college but have nothing to live on if you do?

Now you can.

The most often used disparaging commentary against UBI is it will make people lazy, wanting something for nothing. Instead of seeing it as a way to free people to explore their potential and make not only their lives better, but other people as well through their innovations. If you are no longer trapped by poverty, or even the threat of destitution if you quit your job, you are now free to become yourself to your fullest potential.

And yes, a few may choose to do nothing. But, that also goes for the idle rich, the only difference between the top 1% and someone living on the streets is money. One is admired for their laziness, the other condemned, and even though their actions are exactly the same, the end results are entirely different.

So, before you decide to abandon me and our revolution, take a minute and think to yourself, if I had a guaranteed income, well below rich but enough above homeless, what would I do with that opportunity?

Nice thought, isn't it?

Now... what do you say? Still on board with me?

Then let's go on to *Taxes*.

Only 10 more chapters to go. It's a lot to fix, isn't it?

CHAPTER THREE
TAXES

Oh, taxes. The thing we all agree we love to hate. Except, taxes are the engine that drives our country, without them, the nation can't fund the thousands of services we use and depend on every day. We may hate the idea of paying taxes, but we would hate to lose all the things taxes bring us if they were lost more.

I believe the biggest problem is when we think of taxes we can clearly see on every paycheck money being taken out, but because tax money is so integrated into our daily lives, we don't see the things they support. We don't think about taxes when we turn on the water or drive on our roads or fly in an airplane or cross a bridge or take medication or visit a park or any of the hundreds of things we do all every day, and think, "Thank you taxes for paying for all of these things I enjoy." or even, "I helped make this possible."

But we notice the failings every time a bridge collapses, we drive over a pothole, drink contaminated water, take an unsafe drug, find litter in our parks, we pay attention only when those services are cut back or completely gone. And then, we freak out. "*How could this happen?*", as things, once taken for granted, are gone. And the answer is, we didn't pay for them to continue when we demanded lower taxes.

It's okay to hate them. The same way you hate going to the dentist to get a tooth repaired, a slightly painful event that prevents long term harm. We may hate it, but we also know if we don't go the long term harm can be fatal, so we go and do what needs to be done, even if we hate it.

Now, before I do anything as radical as take your money, we need to talk about how we go about deciding who/what gets money, and what doesn't. I don't mean, let's go line by line through the current tax code, neither one of us has that kind of time, and honestly, isn't useful to what I'm talking about anyway.

What I'm talking about is deciding where our priorities are as a nation, and paying for those things appropriately. To address this, once every 3 years every person 16 and up in America will be given a survey where they rank what is most important to least important in our general budget, something Congress has to consult and use as a basis for budgeting. Which by the way, we will do every 3 years as well. Needing to think things out in advance, and not allowing Congress to leave the building once every three years until they can come up with, and agree to, a workable budget would add a great deal of stability to our country. (Don't worry, we'll feed them, I'm not a monster. But they can only order from Domino's because I do have a little bit of a mean streak.)

We all know generally what is in our national budget, everything from paying teacher's salaries to buying bombs and everything in between. For the survey, we break it down into individual categories, Military, Health & Human Services, Education, Infrastructure, Government Contracts, etc. And then further break it down into subcategories until they can go through the survey in manageable chunks of 10. Every citizen is required to respond and given 2 months to do so, under penalty of law if they fail to return a completed survey. (Waivers can be given for advanced age, infirmary or debilitating illness) They can answer the survey questions online and our answers automatically entered. Once all the data is entered, Congress will have a snapshot of our priorities as a nation and have no excuses to ignore us or pander to the more extreme among us.

But, before anything can be added to the budget, all amendments will have to go through an 80/20 review. Any item added to the possible budget has to show it will benefit 80% of the people and can benefit an individual, corporation, or investment group no more than 20%. So, if a new contract with a corporation is added, it has to show it will help 80% of the general population or 80% of the region it will impact, and only 20% of the benefits can go to the corporation, if not, the contract will be scrapped until a better deal is offered.

We should all enjoy the benefits of our tax spending, it is our money after all being spent. I may be dictator, but this is a democracy I'm ruling over, and it should always be *We the People,* first and foremost or else we need to come clean and call it what it is, an Oligarchy, which would mean our revolution was all for nothing.

INDIVIDUAL & CORPORATE TAXES

Before we begin, first let me say, read this all the way through before you freak out my little revolutionary buddies. When first looking at the tables, you might wish to abandon me to my fate, but you've stuck with me this far, so keep the faith and read ahead.

First, we need to restructure our tax brackets. Going forward, this will be the federal tax rate for all individuals and corporations.

Tax Table

$0 - $10,000	0%
$10,0001 - $25,000	10%
$25,001 - $50,000	20%
$50,001 - $100,000	30%
$100,001 - $250,000	40%
$250,001 - $500,000	50%
$500, 001 - $1 million	60%
$1 million to $2.5 million	70%
$2.5 million - $5 million	80%
$5 million & above	90%

Now, before everyone starts to really freak out over this, each of these brackets applies to all the money you make. Let's say you make $75,000 a year. Starting January 1st, until you hit $10,000, no taxes are taken out of your paycheck. You are free and clear baby, recoup some of those winter holiday expenses you went overboard on, enjoy! But when your gross net income reaches $10,001 you start paying 10% into the system, and when it hits $25,001 you start paying 20% and so on, so you only pay the top bracket in your income level by the end of the year. It's a progressive tax system that rewards work without penalizing poverty.

Oh, I should also mention, no more tax returns. Since it's progressive and comes directly out of your check you pay what you pay, no more, no less. On the bright side, no more filing taxes, paying a tax service, gathering receipts or worrying about an audit if you made a mistake.

If you are self-employed, you can send in your earning quarterly or yearly, it's entirely up to you and whichever is easier for you to calculate. If you own a small business, with fewer than 5 employees and/or make less than $250,000 a year you can choose quarterly or yearly for your business income. Dealer's choice, and whichever helps you out more. Your employees will pay using the above chart per paycheck. You may want to hire an accountant to help you navigate, but my goal is to make paying taxes as simple and painless as possible, like a good dentist. Businesses over 5 employees and/or more than $250,000 will file quarterly.

Now, if you are a corporation, LLC, a shop owner with 5 or more employees, etc the tax code will be slightly different. The same rates apply to your profits, after excluding worker's wages, any investments you make in your workers, building, expansion, and investments in your community can all be deducted from your gross income calculations.

The point of this is to encourage companies to invest in both their workers and in the communities they have settled in. If a company offers free daycare to their employees, it can be deducted. If they choose instead to buy back their own stock, that is not deductible. It makes being selfish less profitable. If you pay yourself a higher salary to offset your business taxes, you'll make it up by paying taxes from your personal income. Businesses, corporations, CEO's, executives, and stockholders will no longer be allowed to exempt themselves from paying into the system that helps support them.

Let's discuss non-profits for a few minutes before we move on. When you think "non-profit" the first thing that pops into your head is probably they work as a charity or something similar to it, and some of them do. But, and I want to stress this, not all of them do. The NFL is a non-profit. Let that sink in, a corporation that rakes in billions every year is structured as a non-profit, even though it clearly shows a massive amount of profit every year. Just doesn't seem right, does it?

I agree, it's not. So, remember the 80/20 rule from earlier?

From this day forward, any company claiming non-profit status has to follow that rule to be considered non-profit and show 80% of the benefits will go back to the community or improvements in the general social welfare. They can keep 20% of the profits for administration, overhead, etc. but anything beyond 20% has to be used to benefit their community, their employees or improvements in the general social structure, but it cannot be used to line the pockets of the owners. If you're going to present yourself as a charity, you are going to act like a charity, or you're going to be required to restructure your company to reflect what you are, a for-profit entity.

Also, to be considered a non-profit, there can be no stockholders nor stocks issued for that company. Short-term investors are allowed if you are a start up and under 3 years old, but you will be required to have all investors paid back by year 5 and no new investors allowed after your second year after applying to be a non-profit.

State, Sales Tax, and Property Tax

I'm going to stay general here, and of course, I will be looking for additional input from advisers on specific details, but here are some of the basic proclamations I, as your humble dictator, will be issuing.

Tax Table

$0 - $25,000	0%
$25,001 - $100,000	10%
$100,001 - $500,000	20%
$500,001 & above	30%

For state taxes, corporate and business exemptions described above will apply here as well. If you invest in your company, employees or communities, you can deduct those amounts from your gross earnings when calculating your tax brackets. Please note, your state taxes will be applied to your gross earning after federal rates have been deducted.

Sales tax help generate additional income for states to provide services to their communities. They are a necessary evil we all participate in to ensure our state can do things for us. But, guidelines should also be given to their amounts and how they can be spent.

Sales tax cannot exceed 7% on any item. No particular group should be forced to carry the burden of any particular industry or to supplement the coffers of the state. It is an undue burden that will end.

Sales tax will be exempt from certain basic living items such as medication, personal hygiene products, food, feminine sanitary needs, diapers, and formula. This list may expand depending on input from advisers.

States cannot give tax break incentives to corporations to bribe them into moving to their state. Nor can municipalities, or cities use tax exemptions as a bribe in any way, such as offering to eliminate property taxes on facilities to entice a business to move to their state or their community.

Sales tax cannot go below 2%, except on exempt items. Your state needs money and we need to keep that in mind while talking about this, so don't cringe too much.

Property taxes I'm not going to make a lot of changes to, at this time. With this caveat, property taxes are to go to public education schools, period. They cannot be used for any other program or used to shore up a shortfall elsewhere in the state or used for private, religious, or charter schools.

In addition, all property taxes will be collected by the state and then distributed to the schools, equally divided using a formula based on the number of students in attendance. It will not matter if you live in a poor neighborhood or a rich one, you will receive the same amount per student for your school.

I will be talking more about this under *Education*.

THE SEPARATION OF CHURCH & STATE

We've all heard about the separation of church & state. We are all also, at least, somewhat aware of the exemptions churches receive, such as property and sales tax exemptions. There has also recently been a great deal of noise about allowing churches to participate in politics. I will be addressing these issues here.

You gotta pay to play. If a church decides to become a political body, they may do so. But, the church will lose all tax exempt status, and will be subject to property tax, sales tax, and taxed on all money brought into the church as income. If a church wishes to enter the secular world, then they will pay the admission fee we all pay to participate.

The 80/20 rule will also apply to all churches. If a church does not qualify under this 80/20 rule they will also lose their tax exempt status. If 80% of the donations received are not used to help their community to provide shelter, care, help or assistance to the needy, it is not a church, they are a for-profit entity and will be taxed as such.

If a church decides to stay out of politics and uses their donations to improve the lives of those they serve, nothing will change. (God) bless and go with (god). (Insert appropriate name of your deity, we're equal opportunity around here)

Now, about all the revenue starting to roll in from churches who no longer qualify for tax exempt status. I have a plan for it as well. All revenue from taxed churches will go into the Universal Basic Income fund. Kicking & screaming against their will, those who claim to be a church, but don't act like a church, will help the general public one way or another, either voluntarily, or through taxes.

And we're back to Universal Basic Income. You've gotten this far so I will assume you, my faithful revolutionary, are still on board with the program. I'm even sure there are a few things you may not wholly like or question, but that's okay, this is a revolution and there's always a learning curve. When new verifiable information becomes available to me, I am always willing to change my mind about something.

But on this, I think this is a good idea. The idea has been around for over 60 years and was originally the basis for Aide to Dependent Family and other social programs designed to help people up out of poverty. This was the holistic response to poverty, but due to political reasons we instead have a piecemeal system that costs a great deal to implement while still allowing millions of Americans to fall through the cracks.

Since its beginning, there have been two schools of thought on how to fund it. Either directly, as we do now for Social Security through payroll taxes or indirectly through general taxation as we do for almost all other programs. As you have been reading through my proposals, I think you've gotten the idea that part of the money will come from general taxation, but the rest will come from investments, like leasing patents generated by tax funded research.

Our initial capital for this program will come from existing funds for the various social net programs and pool all of it together. There will also be a windfall of savings as office buildings are closed down and the process streamlined using only the IRS for tracking and dispersing funds. We'll probably need to add new job slots at the IRS to handle their new responsibilities, but it will primarily be automated once a person is in the system. With another office to track deaths to ensure payments cease at that time.

After that, the government will continue to fund the program through taxes, a percentage of which will come from the dedicated taxes of churches who have elected to participate in our elections or do not meet the 80/20 requirement for non-profit status. A designated percentage of the overall tax intake will be allotted for this program from the taxes you are already paying and will change over time as revenue from investments begins to build up.

We are an innovative society, and we love to make things more cost and labor efficient as we go. It's what we as humans do, and we've been doing it since man first made fire to make their lives a little better. But there is a downside to it, as labor becomes more efficient and technology takes over jobs that once were filled by humans (think switchboard operators if you need a visual) jobs will start to decline.

Lowering the average work week will help with this process and will continue to create employment, for a while. But, if we continue on our current path of progress (unless we blow ourselves up back to the stone age), there's no reason to think automation will do anything more than increase on an exponential scale. We went from the Wright brothers to walking on the Moon in 70 years. We've gone from computers the size of houses to ones that fit into your pocket in even less time. And all of this is wonderful, but it also means before too much longer, the odds are, your job will become obsolete.

I'm not trying to scare you. I am simply sharing with you something science and the tech industry has known about and has tried to share with you. It's going to happen. Unless you have a job that requires daily creativity, in 50 years, it will most likely be gone, replaced by a computer, a program or a bot. And when (not if) that happens, we have two options. Universal Basic Income or the total collapse of our society as we know it. The rich will presumably continue on, at least for a while on the stores of cash and assets they possessed before the financial collapse, but they too will feel it in time. Not even the .01%, in their isolated worlds and almost infinite wealth, can support themselves independently without a society to sustain them.

If 90% of the population is unemployed, replaced by a machine, and with no mechanism to allow them to continue purchasing all the items created by manufacturing or by individuals to sustain life, then our entire economy fails. There is no need to make the next great gadget if no one can afford to buy it. We'll be back to bartering two chickens for a pair of shoes society and hardscrabble living many will not survive.

Universal Basic Income is not about helping out *those people*, but **you**, **your** family, **your** friends, **your** coworkers, and **your** neighbors. You. This will affect every person you know, every industry you've ever heard of, every job you've ever dreamed of, every aspect of your life, your community, and your country will be affected by this. Nothing will be exempt from the transformation that is coming, whether I am dictator or not, as relentless as a nightmare and as unavoidable as gravity.

We can choose to do nothing, stick our collective heads in the sand and say "*no, no, no*" until it rolls over us like a steam engine OR we can head off this disaster and enact UBI for the good of all of us.

But since I'm dictator, I am enacting UBI and will save all of us from this awful fate. You're welcome.

CHAPTER FOUR
HEALTHCARE

Healthcare. We all need it, but we don't all have it, and because of this we are one of the sickest countries in the industrial world. Our life expectancy for the first time ever is going down, not up. We have the highest maternal mortality rates in the industrial world. And the worst outcomes per cost anywhere.

There was a time, in our not too distant past healthcare was not-for-profit. Then, during the Nixon's presidency, he opened the doors allowing for-profit systems to flourish, providing the framework for the healthcare system we have now. It is clunky, expensive, cumbersome, and inefficient, with the goal of profits coming before any consideration of a healthy outcome for individuals.

When people talk about letting the market decide prices, that's easy enough when it comes to things like buying a car or a house, or what you're willing to spend on an evening out on the town. Prices are clearly marked, and you always have the option of choosing not to if you decide it's too expensive. But, when you are in the midst of a medical emergency, you can't shop around for the best price or ask your body to pick a better time to malfunction and put it off until you can afford it.

For that matter, you can't even comparison shop for medical costs, because there is no actual formal cost, it's whatever they decide it's going to be without any oversight or regulations to bring sanity to our medical accounting system. If you called your local hospital today and asked for a quote, for well, anything, the fact is, they won't be able to give you an accurate cost for services, if they agree to give you a price at all. The inmates are running the asylum and there's nothing but chaos anywhere you go.

If you go to a restaurant, they give you a menu, and you pick what you want with the prices plainly stated beside what you are ordering. But when you go to the hospital, it's probably as much as a surprise to them as it is to you when you open the bill. Oh, they'll defend the cost to their dying breath, don't get me wrong, but if you were to ask for the cost of each individual item on the bill, chances are, nothing is going to match, and the answers will change each time you call.

And it's all utterly ridiculous. If the medical world wants to be considered "free market" then they should at least be as bound by clearly defined prices as you would find at say, a grocery store, but they're not. There's nothing "free market" about our system, other than each medical agency is free to decide without regard to actual costs or reality, what to arbitrarily charge you.

So, it is in my humble opinion as your concerned Dictator, we should bring Universal Healthcare to every citizen in our country. And, humble or not, it's what we're going to do, because I'm the dictator, and I get to decide these things.

Listen, I know for many of you this is a scary thing. We have all been bombarded with negative rhetoric about expanding Medicare to cover everyone and how the sky will fall and you will die because of "death panels". But, think about this for a minute, every time an insurance company turned someone down for something medically necessary to keep them alive, what exactly do you think it is but a death panel? It's not Universal Care that gives our nation the dreaded death panel, it's already here, and they work for our insurance companies.

An insurance company's goal is not to provide you with the best care, but to cut as many costs, while charging everything they can in rates, to make their profit margin as high as possible, regardless of the medical outcome their decisions bring. That's the system we currently have. Fewer services, higher costs, and your life in the hands of someone who puts profits before people. So please, don't let the fear mongers scare you with terrible outcomes, because that's what we already have, and they did this to us, eyes wide open, knowing full well they were screwing us over.

It's time we realize the free market is not compatible with healthcare, and not the only way it's ever been done in our country. We had a better way until profiteers stepped in and took affordable healthcare away from us. It is time for us to once again take control of our healthcare services and put people before profits. We don't need to build a new system, we just need to expand what we have to cover all of us. We have Medicare, Medicaid, and Tri-Care (military insurance), we can roll all of them into one, and bring everyone else in under its umbrella.

And yes, it will cost. But we already pay for healthcare in our taxes collectively and to insurance companies individually, and it's costing us dearly. We hear stories every day now about how someone died because they couldn't afford their medication or

IF I WERE DICTATOR

treatment. Of people suffering for years because they couldn't afford to see a doctor. We see the wasteland of suffering our current system has given us, and we can't let the fear of change keep us from doing better, for all of our sakes.

Now, I know there are already plans out there on how to make this a reality, I just need those plans on my desk and a reasonable timeline to institute those changes. So come on my fellow revolutionaries who have shouted the rallying cry of Universal Healthcare for All, step up and help me change healthcare in our country. Please have your plan on my desk at 6 pm the Monday following my swearing in, cuz I know you've got it written out somewhere, right now, just waiting to be read.

Now that I've given the order, I'm sure at least a dozen of those will show up on my desk Monday. We're going to take the best parts of all of your plans and make something workable out of it. I promise.

ACCESS TO CARE

In our country, there are areas underserved by the medical community with limited access to doctors, dentists, or care facilities. Forcing people either to go without care or forced to travel excessive distances to receive even basic general practice care. Between the growing cost of education burdening new doctors with massive debt and the emphasis on profit over people, low-income and rural communities have suffered and gone without.

In later chapters, we will be discussing current student loan debt and expanding free education beyond high school to our citizens. But that's for later, now we will be talking about how to get doctors and nurses into areas that desperately need them.

To begin with, incentives will be given to any doctor who relocates to an area that is without a general practitioner and opens their own medical practice to serve the needs of the community. Additional incentives will be given to provide needed staffing and expansion of services to fill the needs of their community.

When it comes to meeting the needs of our citizens we have a lot to do, but this is a good first step in the right direction. Over the next six years, more targeted medical infrastructure will be added to ensure every citizen can receive, at minimum, basic care at a community level and expanded access as needed outside their community if it's too small to have its own hospital and experts on hand.

I hope the medical community will step up and offer input into these expansion plans and help us create a better future. We all need to pitch in and do what we can to fix what has gone wrong over the years in our relentless pursuit of money over all other considerations. There will be problems as yet unseen as we dismantle the old system and replace it with a new one that put the people first, and will take all of us working together to overcome what we have done to ourselves.

Now that we have our basic healthcare out of the way, let's talk teeth and mental health. When it comes to healthcare, dentistry and mental health have been seen as a separate issue, and yet nothing could be further from the truth.

Without access to dentistry, a person could die from a tooth infection. Or have their entire life ruined because of bad teeth. It lowers their ability to secure a good job or even find a significant other. Our teeth are an important part of our overall health, and will now be included in our Universal Healthcare. Not as a paid for add-on, but as a basic part of our healthcare.

The same goes for mental health services. At some point in our life, we may need to see someone for a variety of mental health reasons. Some people may need short term care, for others, it may be lifelong. But, either way, having an emotionally stable society is a good thing, for everyone.

When it comes to our health, we need to look at the whole person, not just bits and pieces of them while ignoring the rest that have a significant impact on how we live, and even, how long we will live. You're just as dead from an untreated tooth infection as you are from an untreated burst appendix, but until now, one was covered by basic insurance and the other ignored. We fix that now.

I will be addressing the legal status of drugs later on in *Legal Stuff*, but suffice to say for now, when it comes to drug use, addiction will be decriminalized on all levels. Prosecuting someone for a medical problem makes as much sense as punishing someone for having cancer, the harm we cause far outweighs any benefit our society may think we gain from it.

Studies have been done over the last decade have shown us there are better ways to deal with addiction, and now the time has come to update our reaction to those problems.

First, we must understand in a significant number of cases, addiction comes from feelings of isolation, depression, and desperation. Addressing those issues and learning better ways of dealing with a person's inner sense of failure is a far more effective tool in combating addiction than prison time ever could. In fact, punitively punishing someone for addiction only makes the situation worse, since we are only feeding into a person's sense of worthlessness, rather than addressing what brought them to this state, to begin with.

Second, and this may come as a shock to many of you, A.A. and N.A. does not actually work for the majority of the participants. It's one of those pervasive lies we have come to accept as truth, but it still doesn't make it real. It's a pseudoscience, but because of how integrated A.A. is in our culture, few even question its validity in treating addiction. If someone relapses, the system isn't held to account, only the individual for being weak, allowing this less than effective treatment to continue on without question.

With many of the changes coming to our nation, some of the causes of addiction will resolve themselves over time as desperation from an inherently flawed system begin to sort themselves out. But for those who need more immediate help, we need to step up and provide treatment for them, if they want it. But, let me stress here, *if* they want help.

You cannot help someone who does not wish to be helped. You cannot force a person to change against their will. And you cannot force someone to be something they have no desire to be. In our communities, there will always be a small minority of people who simply wish to spend their days in an altered state, and we must respect their wishes to be what they are. In this new country we are creating, all citizens are granted body autonomy, and that means accepting the good with the bad, of that right.

As long as an addict is not harming anyone else or putting their community in danger, they are free to continue the lifestyle they have chosen to live. We don't have to like it, but we do have to accept it. If, on the other hand, an individual puts others in harm's way because of their ill-fated choices, as a community, we have the right to protect ourselves from their stupidity. Addiction services and community service will be a part of it, as well as possible jail time, depending on the nature of the incident. But our laws will no longer reflect punitive punishment, but active rehabilitation for our citizens and we will treat addiction in a similar manner.

When it comes to rehabilitation, there will no longer be two-tiered treatment with high-end care for the wealthy and privileged, and low-end care for those who are not. Rich or poor, all will be treated the same. Nor will we race to the bottom in making treatment equitable, instead we will do our best to give each person the type of care they need, in a safe and secure facility, that does not prey upon a person's fears. They may not be resorts, but neither will they be a prison by another name.

When it comes to alcoholism, there are better treatments out there than A.A. for our citizens. There are new drugs to curb the desire for drinking excessively without having to cut drinking forever and permanently from our lives. Almost nothing we do in life is intrinsically bad, as long as we keep it within maintainable moderation, it is only when we go to excess that problems begin. Teaching moderation is a much more effective tool than preaching total abstinence.

As human beings, we are not perfect, we make mistakes and sometimes use poor judgment, but that doesn't mean we are beyond redemption. When treating our fellow humans, we need to remember we are often just one bad decision from being where they are right now.

For far too much of our history, males have been considered the default parameters for our medical baselines. All of our research, medicine, and treatments are based on what works best for males and then applied to females, with sometimes less than optimal results. We are all one species, but we all have individual medical needs, and it's time our research and applications of treatments reflect this.

I am once again going to bring up body autonomy here. For those who are unfamiliar with body autonomy (ignoring all my previous statements because you skipped ahead), let me quickly explain. An individual has control over who or what uses their body, for what, for how long. Which means, each individual has complete control over their own body, and that right cannot be taken from them by any other person, group, religion, or government. Your body belongs to **You**. No one else can force you to do anything with your body without your permission.

I am going over this right now because it has been a long standing tradition in our nation for a woman's body to be considered not her own. While we've made great strides forward, we still have a ways to go before women enjoy the same level of body autonomy men have taken for granted throughout history. During the next six years, this is something we will be addressing and hopefully, fix before I leave office.

When it comes to medicine, women aren't always seen as the deciders of what happens to them. Doctors will call in spouses, parents, and even consult the law before agreeing to something as simple as sterilization before agreeing to the procedure. Often couched in terms like "For your own best interest" or "You may change your mind in the future" or even "What would your future husband think if you did this?", these statements let each woman know their thoughts on how best to deal with their lives are subject to second-guessing by a host of individuals, and their own decisions may not be honored because of it. Women are treated as secondary to decisions about their own bodies, and this will end. No one knows your own wants, needs, and choices better than you.

And no one should have the power to take your decision out of your hands.

When it comes to other medical treatments, women are often ignored when they go to the doctor and say, "Something is wrong." Even other female doctors put less stock in a woman's discomfort than they do a man's. Part of this comes from cultural conditioning, women are seen as complainers, and men as stoically silent when it comes to general discomfort. And yet, neither science nor sociology back up this almost unconscious stereotype.

Horror stories abound describing sometimes years of debilitating pain that was ignored by a physician only to later discover after persistent complaints, there really was something wrong. Because of the long length of time between first reporting the problem, and actually having a doctor take a woman seriously enough to investigate their concerns, the damage often has increased or become untreatable. This is simply not something that can continue happening to half of our population on a regular basis.

Now, as to how to go about changing the situation, I am open to ideas on how best to combat it. I can see the problem, but as to how to fix it, I am going to need input from people who are more experienced in dealing with this problem than I. So, step up my experts and be heard, now is your time to make a difference in the lives of over 150 million people.

Next, we need to talk about birth control. While birth control should be equally the responsibility of both parties, the fact remains it is women who bear the brunt of the consequences. Becoming pregnant has a multitude of complications attached to it, from maternal mortality rates to standard of living reductions from loss of income during pregnancy and beyond. No woman should be forced to do something they do not want to do, and body autonomy gives them the right to make the choice for themselves. Without interference from parents, significant others, religious groups or the government.

If there are any staunch pro-lifers reading this book, I can feel your blood pressure already beginning to rise, as the sputters of "But, but..." dribble from your lips. You may keep your beliefs without interference, but you will no longer be able to dictate the personal choices of someone else. We are a free country, and that means people are free to do things that cause you no personal harm, even if you don't personally agree with their choices. Body autonomy will always take precedence over another person's personal beliefs in our new system.

There will be no more court battles over another person's body, and no new laws imposed to restrict someone's personal body choices. If someone wishes to try, the court's will respond with "Body autonomy" and throw the case out. There are no more gray areas when it comes to your personal body choices once you've reached the age of maturity. And we'll talk more about it in *Legal Stuff*.

In addition to the above, birth control will be freely available to any who wish it. There will no longer be religious restrictions attached to family planning choices. If you do not wish to use birth control, that is your right, but you are not allowed to take the choice from someone else.

We will also be improving our sex education classes and moving away from abstinence as the only option, to one that encompasses the reality of our bodies and how they function. We will take notes from other countries that have more comprehensive sex education classes that correspond with lower STD and unplanned pregnancy rates.

I'm sure I have made some of you unhappy in this section, and all I have to say is, suck it up buttercup. Freedom doesn't mean you have the right to impose yourself on someone else. Freedom means we each get to make choices based on our own personal needs and desires, as long as they do not interfere with someone else.

I hope the majority of you will continue reading after this chapter. For those who are contemplating throwing this book around the room, take a bit of time and maybe come back to me later. I knew at the start we would not agree with each other all the time, but I hope we can still find our common ground and work together on the things we do agree with each other on.

CHAPTER FIVE
EDUCATION

Education is the cornerstone of any stable modern society and without a well-educated, well-trained population, it will slide into squalor. With the high-tech world continually bringing shiny new toys into existence, to keep up with them we have to have a sufficient number of citizens who understand how to make and maintain them. We cannot continue to compete globally if we don't.

In *Taxes* I discussed changing property tax distribution, so each school will gain an equal share per student. I understand if some of you are horrified by the idea, if you live in a nice neighborhood and pay high property taxes you may feel your children should be the sole beneficiaries of your contributions to education. But, if we are to make the system work for all of us, we have to change, and part of that change is every child, not just yours, is important.

When it comes to college or trade schools we cannot make good, quality education so expensive, so out of reach, for the average student or family, only a small minority can access it. Not if we expect to continue as a first world nation. I don't know about you, but I like new gadgets and tech toys, and I want our nation to become a leader in those areas once again. Because like it or not, my friends, we are no longer seen as the world leader in technology, we have been surpassed by many other nations as our education system has continued its downward slope.

I want the US educational system to be the envy of the world. I want other countries to point to us and say, "That's how it's done!". I want our country to be full of innovators and leaders, full of as much promise as an unopened gift on Christmas morning. I want us to be the country we claim to be, and it begins with education.

Now that I've said all this, we also need to address how we educate and the various forms of education that should be available for our children. We need doctors, lawyers, and scientists that thrive in traditional educational systems. But, we also need mechanics, electricians, and artists who don't. We need a system that nurtures all forms of education, not just traditional white-collar generating ones.

And we need to remove the stigma of going to a trade school rather than a traditional college. Because the last time I checked, your lawyer can't do a damned thing for you if your car breaks down and you need it repaired, other than call a mechanic for you. Trade jobs are as important to the functioning of our society as any doctor, lawyer or scientist is, because, without them, the basic fabric of our society begins to fray if we don't have people to fix or build things. Blue-collar workers play an important role in our society and it's time to stop shaming them for not pursuing a more white-collar career.

Like the saying goes, the fish will always fail if the test is to climb a tree. We all excel at something, the important part is to find what it is and encourage it. But if we are going to insist that the only measure of intelligence is to climb a tree not everyone is going to pass, not because they aren't smart, but because the test was too narrow. Our schools and our classrooms should be designed to encourage children to learn in forms that are best for their age level and interests.

In other changes, our teachers will no longer have to pay out of pocket for the educational needs of their students, it will come from our tax dollars. A school is not just a building to house children while they learn, it is so much more than that, something teachers have always known, which is why they have provided the bright and cheerful learning supplies to decorate each individual classroom and engage their students as much as their budget has allowed.

From here on out, every teacher will be given a classroom budget to cover the expenses for those previously out of pocket purchases. At the end of each semester, teachers will turn in a list of items they need for their classrooms, everything from tissues to tripods, along with their planned activity schedule for the upcoming semester. Each principle will review their plan, then send in a bulk order for the items needed.

We will also be changing our system to year round schooling. First semester will be January, February, March, with April as a holiday month. Second semester will be May, June, July, with August as a holiday month. Third semester will be September, October, November, with December as a holiday month. Breaking up the year in this way has been shown to be beneficial to student's learning. With only a month break between semesters, students don't lose what they have gained, as they generally do during a three month summer vacation. Breaking it up throughout the year

IF I WERE DICTATOR 85

also gives families time to plan vacations outside of the summer months, which is as important as classroom learning in a child's development.

When it comes to our classrooms, innovation will be the key to its development. As part of this plan, I would like our educators to have a greater say in how our classrooms are designed. I would like to encourage active participation from all of our teachers to share their ideas, thoughts, and concerns to be addressed, not only with local school boards, but with other schools across the country. During the vacation time allotted to students, we will institute week long seminars teachers can participate in, and paid for by the school system.

Each semester break, all teachers will choose one (or more if they choose) per seminar to participate in, choosing one that focuses on some area they would like to learn more about or speak at. This would not just be a local thing, but something that spans the country, and each county district hosting an event in city/town rotation to encourage nationwide participation by teachers from all walks of life to share and discover new ways to teach our children.

I would also like to see a program to send some of our educators to other high ranking countries such as Norway to learn more about how their systems work and bring those ideas back, to integrate into our school system. (If you're wondering why I pick Norway so much it's because they are ranked highest in most areas for overall health, happiness and education.)

Teachers, I want you to know, as your dedicated Dictator, how important you are. Without you, our schools could not function. You are the single greatest asset to our educational system, and you should be rewarded equitably for all you have done and will continue doing in the future for our country. As educators, your place in our society should be one of admiration. Shaping young minds to later become functional adults is not for the faint of heart, you are the strength and foundation for all our country's achievements. You are heroes, each and every one of you. It's not a job I could do. I'm good at many things, but teaching is not one of them.

Because I recognize the importance of what you do, most of you will be given a raise. How much you ask? That, I can't tell you yet, but I will no longer allow our teacher to struggle from month to month or live in poverty. So, know a raise is coming, as soon as we can get the funding for our schools settled and the new income system in place. I pledge to you, we will take care of you as you have taken care of our children, and I thank you for all you have done and continue to do on our behalf.

When it comes to the old educational system, I'm tired of our country beating a dead horse over and over again and expecting different results. The horse is dead, it's time to move on. The way we have been running our educational system has not been working, so instead of continuing to double-down on policies that are clearly not working, it's time to do something different. So, I hope you're all in this with me, because educating our children should be a top priority, not only for those who have children, but for every person that lives in our country. If we want to be the best in the world, it begins with education.

Also, the world is **not** flat!

PRIMARY SCHOOL

Primary school should be a time for exploitative learning, not sitting quietly in rows. Young children learn by using their hands and discovering the world in a tactile manner rather than by learning things by rote. It has been a mistake for us to try and force children to learn in a way that is not natural to them, to take the joy out of discovery and put our world into classified boxes. We stifle their enthusiasm for learning when we do these things and I believe we are also damaging their ability to creatively learn in the future as well.

Our country has become too focused on testing our children instead of teaching them how to learn. Which in the long run is much more important than being able to recite a string of lists on demand. The ability to look at the world and discover new ways to do things will serve not only our children, but our society, if we actively encourage future generations to learn, adapt, and use out of the box thinking to solve problems.

In our fumbling attempts to standardize learning, we have burdened our children with far too much homework, burning them out when they should be playing. Later in their education, yes, some amount of homework will become important as they hone their skills through practice to venture forth into the real world, but it's simply not appropriate for a 6 year old.

Primary education should be made up of unstructured play, music, and art. It should be a time to encourage cooperative sharing and learning about numbers, colors, and letters through interactive play activities. Each learning activity should be taught in a way that is entertaining, such as match games, word rhyming, number songs, learning limericks, color quests, becoming more sophisticated as they age. Until middle school, there should not even be desks in the classrooms, but play mats, pillows and soft surfaces for them to sit on, and each classroom should be bright, cheerful and full of things for them to explore and learn from. It is our job as a society to ensure our children, all of our children, receive the things they need to learn and grow, so they can become participating citizens in our society when they reach adulthood.

Along with getting rid of homework for this age group, so too will we be getting rid of testing. We are no longer going to allow teaching for the purpose of passing tests, but teaching for the sake of understanding.

MIDDLE SCHOOL

Our kids are growing up, see how big they've gotten? (Smile indulgently at the little tikes) Middle school will begin their more formal education, a time for desks and a bit of home studying. But, it will also continue with many of the hands on activities from primary school in a more structured manner. Reading and math will become a more central part of their education, with all other activities stemming from those two fundamentals.

Reading for fun and enjoyment will be encouraged, with a variety of reading materials and age appropriate topics given to each student. Students will be given options for reading assignments, instead of one book for all as has been the custom prior to our new system. We want our children to look forward to curling up with a good book (good by their definition, not a supervising adult) and consider it a pleasurable activity. I want to build a nation of readers, one that goes on beyond the classroom to a lifelong love of books. I want us to do everything in our power to create a lifelong love of learning, and it begins with books.

Math will be the other foundation for our classrooms. Taught not as a static subject, but an interactive one. Our students should start with applicable math, using objects, angles and visual learning to reinforce the lessons. Children should be shown how math is in every part of our lives, and see real-world examples of how math affects their daily life to encourage excitement and curiosity. Math is the foundation of all of our science, using math and applying it to everyday life will lead to greater understanding of the world around them, and why math is important. It is currently taught as a very dry subject that has no connection to the real life, we need to change our approach so they see math as part of their daily world.

The arts will also be an important part of middle school education. Encouraging our student to explore the arts and expand their understanding of the world through different media is important. Education is not about learning one subject and then moving on to another with the first having no relation to the second, but instead, it is one continuous process easily flowing from one area to another. Art and music are often the bridge between the two. There is math in music and in art, teaching them together can help build those connections in young minds.

School wide projects will also be encouraged in middle school as well, not as after school activities, but as part of the curriculum. Projects such as student gardens, where all the children learn how to grow, harvest and then prep and cook what they have grown. Theater productions will become a central part of each semester, with students participating in all aspects of it depending on their abilities, anything from acting to set painting to music, and so on, for the production. The point is to teach life skills, cooperation, math, reading, history, art, science, and music as a whole rather than chopped up skills scattered here and there across their educational landscape.

When our children reach middle school, I want them to be excited about going to school and learning new things. I know I do not have all the answers here, this, like most of the book, is an outline of the path to get us where we want to be. And educators, I need you. I need you to step up and help shape the education system you are a part of, I want your voices to be heard and for you to feel you are a part of something important because you absolutely are.

SECONDARY SCHOOL

Secondary school, where our children are closer to adulthood than childhood, and now is the time to teach them how to become functional adults, with all the responsibilities, complications, and confusion that comes with it. Over the next several years we will also need to address the educational shortfalls inherent in the previous system for teaching our children how to go out into adulthood, preparing them for what is to come.

Our younger children will be much more prepared than our current secondary school students when it comes to life skills, since it will be an integrated part of their education. But for our current, soon to be adults, we'll need to address those shortcomings during the changeover. A comprehensive life skills core class will be integrated into our educational system that will cover such subjects as filling out job applications, cover letter writing, learn about taxes and why they are important to our way of life, budgeting skills and how the stock market works, what credit is and how to manage it without going into debt. All those small things you wish you had learned in high school and became big problems, floundering about learning as adults. With real-life consequences looming over you if you failed to figure it out in time. We want our children to walk into adulthood with confidence, and this will help provide the foundation for it.

Reading and math will continue to be core subjects for all students, as well as more in depth studies into science, history, world and national politics, and the environment. The class structure will be changed as well, more resembling college courses. Classes will be set up into longer block courses, allowing students more time in class with the teacher and less time at home alone learning a subject. School-wide projects will also continue to be an integrated part of the weekly curriculum. With one major change, students can choose each semester which project they wish to participate in. Adding to the options may be an applied science project or a construction project of some kind that changes each semester. The goal is to encourage students to participate in a project in an area that interests them. Each project will require students to start from scratch and create something together to be presented as an exhibit at the end of each semester for parents, other students, and the community to enjoy.

Another change, by the end of the student's first year in secondary school, they will choose between traditional college or trade focused classes. Most teenagers have a general idea of what they would like to pursue as adults, if not the specifics of the field. A student who excels in painting requires a different education than someone who wishes to pursue an education in applied physics. Neither is a bad choice, they simply require a different type of training. During their secondary schooling, students can begin to learn more about the areas that interest them and gain more in depth training in those fields.

During their junior year, students will enter a mentoring program and will include an internship in the field they have expressed an interest in pursuing. If a student is unsure of their choices, they can change the focus of their mentoring program once a semester or can continue until graduation in one particular field. This allows a student to become familiar with the type of career they may spend the rest of their life pursuing. And, decide before it's too late, if it is right for them in reality. If someone wants to be a pediatrician, but finds out sick children make them nauseous, pediatrics may not be for them. It's better to find out before they spend countless hours studying to be a doctor only to discover their inability to actually do the job.

The secondary year of education will be more focused on addressing the individual educational needs of each student as opposed to the one size fits all approach. Students will work closely with school counselors and mentors to tailor their education to achieve their goals. Graduation will no longer be based on a points system, but with the achievement of each individual educational plan designed to give each student a secure foot forward towards higher education or directly into the workforce, depending on their career goals.

When our student graduate, the goal is for each of them to be fully prepared to go on to the next step of their lives as independent adults with confidence.

GRADUATE SCHOOL

In our country, we need an educated population, and the best way to do this is to ensure each child is given the best opportunity to advance their education to the highest level they wish to receive, free individually, and supported by our taxes. It makes no sense that up until now, primary education from Pre-K to 12th has been free in all public schools, but our public colleges are not. That will now change.

If you are a private school, you may continue as you have been, but all public state and community colleges will fall over to the new rules. Some of the new rules may come with a cry of dismay, but the point of a higher education is to educate our students, not pay fat salaries to football coaches or build giant stadiums in effigy to sports enthusiasts. Sports have a place in our society, but they should not be the central concern of our colleges, educating our young adults should be. Some of the costs are generated from attempting to turn our colleges into resorts, with all the amenities, luxury rooms, water parks, and state of the art sports equipment. Oh, and the laser everyone's been talking about over at M.I.T. put on the just gotta have it list.

Each college tends to specialize in some field, activity or point of research to attract the kind of students (and funding) they are hoping to entice. Each school is competitive with every other college in their race to gain who they deem the most prestige, and that translates into ever higher price tags for students. But, unless your college is specializing in advanced scientific research, you probably don't need a state-of-the-art laser for anything but bragging rights.

Our higher education costs have gotten completely out of hand, $25,000 or more per semester, per student, is simply an astronomically out of control cost. But, I guess when you realize there are coaches making over a million a year, and college dorm that look like resorts, then some of it snaps into place, and it's gotta stop. There are other reasons for this out of control skyrocket in graduate schools, and to be quite truthful, a very convoluted list we could wander about for hours in. It's going to take a lot of effort to actually untangle this mess, and I hope, with help, we can get it all sorted out.

We're going to have to scale extraneous back into the world of reality if we are ever going to hope to educate our population without going bankrupt. So, to begin with, there are going to be caps on how much each college will receive per student, and perhaps something to the effect of 60% of their funding is to go directly to student education, and the rest divided up between salaries, sports, campus upkeep, equipment, and amenities. Since those caps per students will be universal to all public schools, it will put most colleges on a fairly level playing field, and now up to the school to draw in students based on the quality of their education, not their yoga classes.

School trustees will most likely be screaming at this point. I'm sorry, but something's gotta give if we are to educate our people, and chasing a ball or luxury rooms aren't going to do that. And honestly, after their year of service, I don't think your students are going to complain too much as long as their rooms are comfortable and the food is edible.

We need to go back to colleges being places of education, not entertainment. And that's not to say entertainment can't be found while away at college, but people are able to create their own past times, the school doesn't need to create all of it for them.

Now that we've talked about traditional college education, let's move on to trade schools. Just as important, often just as expensive. Perhaps, the main reason why trade schools are so expensive is most are privately owned. Only about 30% of trade schools are publicly owned, and most of those, are in association with a community college. We need to increase access to trade school education and fold it into our free higher education blanket. Trades are as important to the general welfare as more traditional colleges, they keep our country running by doing all the jobs needing to be done to keep it from falling apart.

Nurses are just as important as doctors. Mechanics are as important as astrophysics. Architects as important as attorneys. Trade schools produce the makers in our country, the people who take the plans and mold them into reality. Everyone, give 'em a high five for not letting our country fall into ruin, and building and maintaining all the cool stuff we love, like houses, heat & A/C, cars, roads, computers, and the phone we won't let out of our hands. Man! We love that stuff! Now start sharing some love with the people who bring it to us. And let's stop treating their education as "less than" because without them, everything we love will slowly begin to disappear. So, let's make sure we have all those wonderful people and not have them go into lifelong debt to be able to do these things for us.

To start, I believe we need to expand access starting with our local community colleges. Increase their funding to be able to provide training to those going into these fields and allow community colleges to offer a larger diversity of classes. We should also invest in creating more trade school independent of our community colleges to provide even more access for students in all communities.

We also need to discuss already accumulated student debt. We are in a crisis of debt to the tune of 1.3 trillion dollars. All that debt is weighing down our economy and trapping our population is a cycle of debt they may never be free of with the current system. The debt is so great, it is putting off home ownership, marriage, having children, and even going out to eat for an entire generation. It's caused a spike in mental illness as the stress of mountains of debt, often not understood when they signed on the dotted line as a newly made adult, and feeling trapped and hopeless because of it.

We are going to have to bite the bullet as a nation and forgive the debt. To give one generation free education and letting the last suffer under its weight is simply not fair, nor is it good for our country. I know, the 1.3 trillion hit is going to hurt, but it will also come with benefits to our communities and our economy. And while you are looking at that debt, please remember, money isn't real, it's only an accounting system, and most of the money is owed to us anyway, so all we're really doing is forgiving ourselves for our past mistakes and moving on.

There are a lot of things that should be done and could be done to improve our educational system from Pre-K to post graduate schooling and everything in between. Our system has been a mess for a while now, with patchwork quick fixes and throwing lots of money at a problem and hoping something sticks. Our educational system needs to be the centerpiece of our country, because all of our greatness stems from what happens within the hallowed halls of learning. We cannot progress or sustain our country without giving each child the opportunity to learn, thrive and grow into the amazing adults we all know they can be.

Each child is born is full of unlimited potential just waiting for the chance to become. It is our job as adults to give them the opportunity. Raising a child does not rest solely on the shoulders of its parents, but on every member of their community, and our country, working together to ensure each and every child is given a chance.

CHAPTER SIX
HOUSING

Everyone needs a place to lay their head and call their own. It's one of those fundamental things we all need and the touchstone for how well we can cope with the rest of our life. Home is where we sleep, shower, store our things, organize our life, entertain our friends, pretty much everything comes from having a space that belongs to us. It's part of the American Dream, along with the white picket fence, and 2.5 kids running around the yard with a dog, waiting to have apple pie for dessert (please feel free to insert your own version of the American Dream here if this one doesn't work for you).

In our country, there are currently six empty houses for every homeless person, and yet we have both a housing crisis and a homeless crisis. Just thinking about those numbers are enough to make me a little crazy, 18.9 million unoccupied homes, sitting empty, while people freeze to death in the winter because they have nowhere to live. And the problem doesn't end there. Housing prices continue to rise while wages have remained stagnant for over a decade, pricing out people from affordable housing even if they work fulltime. Adding to this whole fiasco, the banks have done their fair share of damage after the housing bubble popped and the emergence of auto-foreclosures in the wake of the catastrophe they created out of greed.

We have entire areas of our country that are wastelands of empty houses and closed businesses. A tumbleweed rolling down the middle of the road would not be out of place in one of these areas. As these neighborhoods stagnate, the remaining few evacuate if they can, in search of a more viable area to live, in the hopes of a better life. Those who can't, are forced to deal with a lack of services, jobs, and opportunity, often falling further into poverty, lost and forgotten.

When it comes to housing, we need to address not only getting a person into a place, but also the problems contributing to the housing crisis that got us to where we are now.

There are four main things we need to do to fix our housing

problems. One, we need to get people off the streets and into homes. Two, we need to make sure people have access to affordable housing once they are off the streets. Three, we need to encourage home ownership for those who want it. And finally, fourth on our list, we need to revitalize abandoned areas to encourage people to move into those neighborhoods once again.

I have some ideas of how we can do all of these things, but again, I am also going to need help. I'm going to need city planners, housing specialists, community organizers, and poverty experts to jump in and help me create a sustainable solution that benefits all of us. I'm open to suggestions and modifications to my ideas, as long as the long term outcome is getting all our people into affordable housing.

So, come on people, we can do this!

ADDRESSING HOMELESSNESS

We currently have over a half a million people, a quarter of which are children, living on the streets. Those are numbers we should all feel ashamed of, god knows I do, which is why I have taken in so many over the years. But, even as your beloved Dictator, I can't take them all in personally, so we're going to have to do this wholesale.

Now, before we begin, I want to address a few things about being homeless. One, very few are homeless by choice. I have known exactly one, ONE, in all my years on earth who was homeless by choice. His name was Shawn, he lived in Phoenix and was a day laborer on construction sites. He'd come by my home a few times a week for a meal and a hot shower, hang out for a while and then head back out as the mood struck him. So, I will admit it is possible that a very small minority are actually homeless by choice. But for all the rest, it is usually a combination of poverty, housing shortages, and skyrocketing rent prices that lead to them living on the streets.

Two, it is almost never because a person was lazy that they're on the streets. Around 45% of all homeless work, another 25% are children, 24% are the elderly, the remaining are suffering from untreated mental illness. Our vets make up a decent chunk of that percentage as well, it's estimated 39,471 vets are homeless on any given night, 70% of which suffer from combat related injuries or PTSD.

Three, the homeless do not deserve to be left on the streets or treated as less than human. Many of the policies in the past concentrated not on how to fix the problem, but instead, focused on ways to make the homeless even more miserable. Putting spikes in areas where they shelter. Taking away their blankets or camping equipment during the winter. Creating laws that make it illegal to feed the poor. Their lives are already hard enough, why have we felt the need to make it worse? To that, I honestly have no answer. I cannot put myself into a mindset where I take joy or satisfaction from another person's suffering, so it will remain a mystery, at least to me. I hope, if you are reading this book, you are equally as clueless, then again, I can't imagine someone who takes satisfaction in sowing suffering reading this book either. But, just because we can't figure out those people it doesn't mean we can't do something to fix this situation despite all their protests. I am Dictator after all, I can do what I want.

So, how are we going to end homelessness? Get that person (or family) a home! Sounds simple, doesn't it? Well, it is. And it's a program that has been used in various cities on a small scale throughout the world with great success. Now, we need to take this concept and spread it nationwide.

Once a person is off the streets and becomes registered for their UBI, the problem will begin to sort itself out. But first, we have to find them and get them somewhere safe. To that end, we are going to need caseworkers. Since we closed down of many social net programs, perhaps the people who worked in those jobs could be moved over to this new project, it's almost a perfect solution now that I think about it.

A caseworker's job will be pretty straightforward, find the homeless, put them in housing, and once they are in housing, address what each person needs to thrive. Help them set up their UBI, find a job, mental health support, medical needs, help enroll them in college or trade school, or whatever an individual needs to begin getting their life in order. A caseworker will work closely with their clients for the first three months they are off the streets, and if a caseworker deems it necessary, they can continue for another three months. If further assistance is needed, that person can be transferred to a more sustainable case manager trained in special needs. The goal is to help each person feel safe, secure and stable in a home they can call their own.

The next on the list is where we will find those homes for them to feel safe, secure, and stable in. Homeless shelters are not a solution to the problem, only a quick fix with no good long term benefits. It has been our standby option, and while it does help some get off the streets for a night or two, it is not designed to do much more than give people a meal and a bed for a night. So the answer is, the government rents them. Each caseworker will be given a list of available housing in their area and will use the list to place each person or family into appropriate housing, and for the first three months, the rent will be covered by federal housing funds.

The housing list will be made up of a mix of government

housing, and property owners who comply with federal housing regulations and agree to accept payments as negotiated as reasonable for their area. All housing units will meet basic living standards, with working heat, water, and appliances, and kept in good repair. Slumlords need not apply (and I'll be discussing them a little later on). Before any location can be put on the list, an inspection will be made of the property to ensure it meets basic living standards. If the property does not, the owner will be cited and required to make all necessary repairs, whether they stay in the program or not. Periodic random visits will be made to each location for as long as those properties remain on the approved list.

Another aspect of this problem we need to address is youth homelessness. Not all those children living on the streets come accompanied by adults. Many are out on the streets because they have been kicked out of their homes or because of abuse or drug use in the home, the death of their only caregiver or a number of other problems have left them alone, vulnerable, and easy prey to predators. They have opted for the streets because neither foster care nor institutional living has any appeal, and after going through the foster care system myself, I can't say that I blame them.

But we do need a solution, one that gets them off the streets but doesn't put them into a worse situation than they were in before. One possible solution is youth hostels. They would be placed in government owned apartments designed to take in youth capable of mostly independent living. Each floor would have a counselor to help them navigate into adulthood in a safe environment where they could still retain reasonable control over their lives. Each youth would receive their own apartment, free of charge, and a small living stipend to cover their basic living expenses such as food, clothing and other necessities. If they have siblings, they will be kept together, and additional support services will be given to help them remain together. Re-enrollment in school will be encouraged and services, such as tutors, will be provided with additional support to help get them back into school.

Every floor will have its own live-in counselor, trained to help these youths thrive in their new lives off the streets. They will help arrange counseling, assess medical needs, drug counseling, and arrange support services they deem appropriate. Their job is not to contain them, but support them in a safe and secure environment so they no longer feel the need to run. If it is possible to reunite a youth with their estranged family, that too will be encouraged, but not required as part of the program.

Appropriate relocation will also be assessed as they come into the system. If prior to being placed in a hostel they were involved in gang related activities, prostitution or other illicit activities, it may be in their best interest to be moved to another area of the country where they have no connection with their prior life. Giving them a true clean start, away from fear of reprisal. Each youth will be given an intake interview to address this and other potential problems, but each youth will also be given options on how they wish to proceed. Their lives up to this point have been largely dictated by the whims of others without their input, so giving them some feeling of control will be a must in this program. The more control they feel they have, the less likely they will be to bolt or even hide from help while still on the streets.

My goal in all of this is to bring down homelessness down to as close to zero as possible, as quickly as possible. And with your help, I know we can do this.

AFFORDABLE HOUSING

Affordable housing is equally important. There could be a thousand houses for every person who needs one, but if they are priced so high no one can afford them, it immediately becomes self-defeating. So, as your dedicated Dictator, I'm going to do something that is going to make some people scream (cover your ears everyone, it's going to be very loud around here for a bit). I'm going to regulate rent prices.

Currently, there is nowhere in our nation where someone working full-time minimum wage can afford reasonable housing. I have, as your loving Dictator, increased minimum wage, but that still puts much of the housing out of reach for people. Something as basic as housing should be affordable and within reach for anyone. The rising cost of housing has far outpaced the rise of income, resulting in either abandoning people to the streets or so in debt just trying to keep a roof over their head they slip a bit more behind each month. I plan on changing that.

Government housing is one solution. Maybe not the best, but it may be one of the fastest to meet the needs of those on the lower income scale. And, I'm not talking about the slums we now have with their bottom of the barrel, rat warren gloom. Living in a place that projects hopelessness does not help our cause, and does not help those who live there. So first, we tackle existing government housing and work to improve it.

Inspectors will go out and assess each housing unit and make a list of everything that is wrong, and cost projections to fix everything. If the building is beyond reasonable repair, then we're gonna have to build another. If the inspector finds the cost to repair is less than a whole new building complex, then repairs will begin as soon as is reasonably possible.

A few thoughts on these housing complexes. It's not enough to just have running water and heat, and while those things are important, these buildings need to be more than hovels if we are going to bring everyone up to a decent standard of living. Hopelessness breeds more hopelessness, giving us a vicious cycle of generations of people living in despair with no hope for anything better. We can, and will, do better.

As part of this program, I would like residents as involved in the projects as is reasonable. I would like their ideas and their needs taken into account during the planning stage and employment opportunities given to the residents as priority hiring for those projects. Building managers will be full time residents of the building and grounds maintenance staff will be hired from within the building.

Each building will be retrofitted with new green tech, and I'm going to insist these housing units become marvels of clean energy. Each unit will be updated with energy efficient windows and appliances, and safe plumbing and electrical wiring. Other additions to improve quality of life will be, one floor set up as a community daycare center free to each resident and staffed with trained daycare workers. Each complex will provide community gardens, a small park with playground equipment, and other reasonable amenities to bring hope to these communities.

In the next chapter, I will be discussing large scale community gardens to address food deserts in our country. I would like to encourage these two programs working together to build stronger communities. But we will talk more about it in the next chapter.

Each new building will be created using as much green tech as is commercially possible and our government housing complexes to set the standards for green living for the rest of the country. I want our low-income housing to be a shining example of everything we can be as a community, and as a country. Everything I talked about in *The Environment* should be a part of the new housing we are going to build. We have to start somewhere, and this seems like as good a place as any.

Rents will be set at 25% of each unit's net income. To gain entry, you must be low-income, but once in, you may remain as long as you wish, but rent will always reflect income.

The next step up from government housing, is of course, privately or bank owned rentals. (I wonder if they've stopped screaming yet?) As I stated before, I will be instituting rent control. But, I'm not going to make any sweeping statements as to how it should be calculated, for that, I'm going to rely on experts to help create a reasonable formula to help people attaining housing without gouging building owners. I am not without sympathy for building owners need to make a profit, or have enough funds in reserve to fix any problems with their properties. A balance must be struck between the two needs that are reasonable to everyone.

So, I will now ask people who have backgrounds in community planning, poverty experts, housing experts, and others in related fields to step up and help design the framework for this. In six months I want to see a workable proposal on my desk, and we will begin implementation shortly thereafter.

As part of this plan, there will be new standards for housing. Slumlords will no longer be allowed to flourish in our country. All housing will be expected to maintain a safe and secure environment for their tenants, and if an owner refuses to bring their properties up to the new standards, their properties will be forfeited to the government to become part of our government housing initiative or torn down if it deemed a loss. Any property that is deemed a loss, appropriate housing for that area will be built to replace the structure that was torn down. Nor will slumlords be rewarded for their greed, if a property is forfeited they cannot claim it as a loss and hope to recoup their losses.

If a property owner wishes to bring their buildings up to standard, but cannot afford it, low-interest loans will be provided to the owners. As part of this program, they will give preferred status to low-income families or individuals after the repairs are complete. They will also be required to become part of the rehoming project to end homelessness for as long as they own that building.

Another practice I want to end is empty buildings used as tax shelters. Purchasing housing as capital investments and left empty, used only for the purpose of tax shelters needs to end, or at least be brought down to reasonable levels. The current system has resulted in skyrocketing rental costs as properties are pulled off the market to only stand empty while people desperately search for housing. If a bank takes possession of a house, they will have six months to either sell it or rent it, or forfeit it to the government. For individuals, well, I'm going to rely on my experts to decide the best course forward to deal with the glut of empty investment homes. We will all do our part in helping to end this manufactured crisis.

HOME OWNERSHIP

Home ownership is not for everyone. There are some who prefer apartment or rental living for a variety of reasons, and I respect that. Caring and maintaining a home can be expensive, and not everyone shares my enthusiasm for remodeling projects. I get it. But, for those who do want to own a home, we need to work on bringing this dream to reality without burdening people with unreasonable interest rates and hurtles designed to bring about failure so the banks can snatch those homes back and resell them for additional profits.

The 2007 housing bubble fiasco was primarily caused by greed from the banks. They pushed loans they knew people couldn't afford, knowing, either way, they'd come out ahead, leaving families in devastating debt whatever the outcome. To help combat this, there will be caps on how much interest a bank will be able to charge for a mortgage, it will never again reach the loan shark levels of the past. Another rule I am considering is holding the banks accountable if they engage in shoddy loan practices. If a bank issues a loan by playing fast & loose with the rules, if the mortgage holders are swept underwater as part of the loan design, the bank will be forced to reduce the interest rate to 3% and reduce the mortgage amount owed to the bank by half. I will not allow banks to be rewarded for unethical practices.

Yearly audits on all mortgage loans will become a standard practice to keep bad faith loans in check. We will be implementing new regulations on banks, since they can't seem to do a decent job of behaving themselves without oversight. In the past, every time we have loosened regulations on the banks they have paid us back by crashing our economy. We will not fall into the habit again of believing the banks when they promise to be good, because history has shown us over and over again, they cannot be trusted when left to their own devices.

New rules will be implemented to encourage home ownership, but no longer will banks be allowed to push loans that are outside of a family's ability to afford by using creative numbers or lifetime mortgages to bring it down to "affordable" rates. Nor will a home loan be issued if the monthly loan amount exceeds 30% of the client's net income. There will also be new rules if a family falls on hard times to help them navigate through a crisis without losing their home.

One will be forbearance. If the family experiences a financial collapse and a loss of 50% or more of their income, they can ask for a year forbearance on their mortgage. During that year the bank will work with the family to restructure their loan to keep their home.

If it is not reasonably possible for them to keep their home, I would like to see a program put in place for home swapping. A bank can help negotiate a mortgage trade with families who are looking to trade their smaller home and lower mortgage for a larger home and higher mortgage. Eviction will only be the option of last resort.

I am also open to other ideas to making home ownership more attainable. But I never again want our country to suffer as it did when the banks gambled with people's lives and called it a good day.

Revitalizing our neighborhoods is as important as getting people into homes. Broken neighborhoods with streets in need of repair, limited access to shopping areas, few job opportunities, and despair seeping around every corner is not good for either individuals or communities.

I plan on using the Year of Giving as part of the plan to combat this. Our nation's youth will go into these areas and clean them up, plant gardens, and help support new services I plan on bringing to each of these areas.

These communities will also be given priority in city maintenance plans. Targeting issues, such as repairing roads, water and sewer services, mass transit, and upgrading the electrical systems for more solar and wind initiatives.

Getting jobs into these neighborhoods will be crucial for revitalization. And the best way to do this is to encourage small businesses to set up shop in underserved communities. Low interest loans and other considerations will be given to people who wish to open a business, with priority given to those who are residents of that community.

I would like city planners to work with local residents to bring in the kind of services and businesses each community needs to thrive. Using local, state and federal money, we will build up our communities and improve living conditions for all of our citizens. Living in low income areas will no longer mean being resigned to broken homes, stagnating communities, and a lack of opportunities.

As part of these programs, community centers will be built and become a central part of each neighborhood. After school programs for youth. Cultural programs such as art, music, culinary classes, dance, and book clubs, for youths and adults. Other activities could be live bands, art shows, book and poetry readings featuring local musician, artists, and writers. Community involvement is essential to what we are trying to accomplish. When communities come together, it is easier to identify with each other, breaking down divides that come from isolation. Here too we can use our Year of Service youths to help create and serve in these community centers.

We've made a mess of our country and our communities, abandoning areas as the buildings aged and leaving them to decay as businesses and people moved on. They are an eyesore to the public, and often dangerous places as the buildings become more unstable with age. They discourage new businesses from entering and bring down property values. It's contributed to the creeping urban sprawl as people move ever outward away from these discarded places, encroaching on farmland, parks, and undeveloped areas.

We will reclaim the industrial areas that have gone to ruin and left abandoned. Projects will be created to tear down these eyesores and create new living areas or let them become parks, areas for solar or wind generation, hydroponic gardens, or even reseeded with local plant life and left to go back to natural areas of green. Whichever serves the community best.

Making our communities clean and green is an interwoven thread in everything we are trying to do. During my Dictatorship, I will work diligently to end the creeping rot of our inner cities, not with austerity but with programs designed to breathe new life into these forgotten areas. Every individual, family, community, and city is important to our country, leaving areas behind to suffer while others enjoy a multitude of favor will no longer be tolerated.

We teach our children when they are young that sharing is caring, yet we forget those values as we grow older. Our care for one another should not end at family and close friends, but to include strangers who walk alongside us in life as well. We need to start seeing ourselves, not divided by wealth or location or status, but as a collective whole we all depend on every day, even if we don't see it, it's there, keeping the wheels running and the country moving.

When we raise up others, we raise up ourselves as well.

If you want, you can use these blank pages to write notes.

CHAPTER SEVEN
FOOD

Food, the third most important thing in our lives, only behind air to breathe and water to drink. (Even if it's 7th on my list) It is a basic need each and every person partakes in if we wish to survive.

The cost to end world hunger has been estimated at $30 billion a year. It's a lot of money, but considering how much has been spent for less noble causes, it shouldn't cause us to pause as we consider how to get food to those who need it the most. We have the means to feed every hungry person in our country, what we have lacked up until now is the will to do so.

One of the biggest problems we have is food waste. Between 30% and 40% of all food produced in the United States is wasted. That comes out to $161 billion in wasted food each year. Suddenly that $30 billion doesn't seem so large, does it? Much of it is wasted before it is even sent to markets, sent to landfills instead of grocers. Supermarkets also have a hand in food waste, many refusing to put out produce that has a minor blemish or bruise, preferring to throw edible food away than put in on a shelf for sale. And of course, individual households allowing food to go bad before getting around to eating what we've bought adds to our overall waste. (I've been guilty of this as well, but we can all do better.)

We have become far too comfortable with throwing away editable food. Preferring to allow people go hungry, and letting meat and produce to go a landfill rather than share what we have. The justifications for our actions are many, but they are nothing more than excuses to make ourselves feel better, preferring to blame the hungry rather than the system that allows it to continue.

Another part of the problem is what farms produce. Our nation subsidizing industrial farming of corn, soybeans, wheat, and milk contributes to lots of food being produced, but not enough getting to people who are hungry. And while all of those things can contribute to eating, much of it is not produced for individual consumption by consumers.

Gone are the days of sustainable, multi-produce variety farms. Instead, as you travel through our farmlands you see vast seas of wheat, corn, and soybeans barely broken by a tree, much less a tomato plant. And transporting all those perishable goods all over the United States bring their own set of problems and expenses. Most large cities are only three days away from starvation if anything happens to disrupt incoming food shipments, and rarely do we think about where our food comes from, until suddenly the shelves are bare after a disaster.

Feeding our nation isn't so much a matter of money or food production, it's a matter of what we are going to do about it. I have ideas (don't I always?) on what we can do about this. Some will be radical, others nothing more than minor tweaking of the existing system. But, of course, as always I will be looking for input, from farmers, food specialists, nutritionists, agriculture specialists and others associated with our food crops and feeding people.

Currently, 1 in 7 in our nation lives in food insecurity. That number is far too high for a nation that produces as much food as we do. Working together we can fix this.

FOOD DESERTS

If you're wondering what a food desert is, it's an area, often in inner cities, that have limited or no access to fresh foods or produce. Approximately 20% of our population live in an area considered a food desert, and around 82% of them are from low-income urban areas.

To fix this, we need to change how we think about getting food to those areas. As I mentioned before, transporting food is one the biggest costs associated with getting food to our tables. So, this is my proposal, we bring the farms to the people, in the form of hydroponic and container gardens.

I hereby charge, as your caring Dictator, the Agriculture Department to begin development of sustainable hydroponics and container food production throughout our nation in the form of community gardens. Each community garden will be charged with growing enough food to sustain the population around it. Each community garden will grow a variety of foods, based on local consumption and need to ensure a healthy diet. Other things that might be added to the facilities are fish farms, goats, to make local cheeses and curds, and even chickens added for both their meat and their eggs. Each community will have a say in what goes into their gardens and each garden facility should be flexible enough to change and adapt to the needs of their community.

Now, this does a number of things that will spread out beyond food consumption, affecting job growth, employment, and local economies. Because not only will these facilities grow food, but we will need infrastructure associated with them to distribute what is grown and people to work them.

Each garden facility will also have a grocer associated with it and everything they produce will be available for sale. Other non-local basic needs and food items can also be included, but the primary focus of each store is to distribute what is produced in the community gardens.

Other requirements, while building the garden local residents must have priority in hiring over non-residents for any job they are qualified for. Each garden will be run by a local community board once it is operational. The community board will not only be in charge of what to grow, but how much is grown and each garden is to keep waste as close to zero as possible, but cannot exceed 5% of total production. Local tastes and preferences are to be used when deciding what is grown, because no matter how healthy something is, if people don't like, they're not going to buy it. Kale comes to mind as I talk about this. Super healthy food, terrible taste that nobody actually likes. But a good mix of fruits, vegetables, and herbs should be maintained.

And while food waste can't be reasonably kept at zero, keeping it from a landfill is. With that in mind, each community garden will be responsible for its own composting. Not only for what is created in the garden, but will also take in local residents' food waste as well. Compost will be given away for free to any local resident and used to help sustain the community garden.

The community gardens should be self-sustaining, once the initial set up is complete. No pesticides will be used, instead, the gardens will rely on companion planting and other organic means to keep the plants healthy. Some plants will intentionally let go to seed to secure the seeds for the next planting. Community gardens may also exchange seeds between the facilities if they wish to diversify to meet the changing needs of their communities.

I look at these community gardens as incubators for economic development, particularly in low-income areas devastated by closing industries that once sustained them. Providing each community with employment and empowerment to build a better future.

As these gardens grow, I would like to see the community grow around them with other small associated businesses such as cafes, restaurants, bakery's, and pubs. To encourage this, once a garden becomes operational and producing goods, grants can be applied for to start these kinds of enterprises by local residents based around local cuisine and what is produced in their community garden.

To gain one of these grants they must comply with certain regulations. At least 70% of the menu must come from their local garden. The person applying should be a resident from within that garden's area for at least 1 year. They must agree to hire only local residents and they cannot at any point sell their business without the consent of the local growing board. Nor can it be associated with or come under the control of any chain. Once a grant is obtained, funds will be given to help with start up operations and to help cover losses for the first year as they build up patrons. If they cannot make it profitable after a year, they have the option of either going it alone to try and keep it operational or they can turn it over to the local community board and walk away.

These gardens will provide steady and dependable employment, run, not by profit-centered CEO's, but by the communities themselves. Each garden will be given the means and the tools, in the beginning, using federal funds to support them, but over time, would become independent employee owned operations, feeding and sustaining their own communities.

FARMS

Farming has been the backbone of our nation since we became a nation. But over time, many of our farms turned into industries, producing not goods for food consumption but for commercial consumption. Through bribes, the government of the past encouraged farmers to move away from sustainable, multi-produce production, to single crop growing, like corn.

This is not good for our economy, for our environment or the family farmer. Putting all their proverbial eggs in one basket means if their one crop has a poor yield, it could wipe out everything for that farmer. It has also encouraged the growth of corporate farms over family farming, often to the detriment of the communities they settle in. If you want a good example of this, think industrial hog farming. If you've ever driven by one, much less been forced to live next to one, you know exactly what I mean. If not, just think of living next to an open sewer that occasionally rains poop down on your house and you get the idea.

So, to combat this, I offer a new bribe to our farmers. Change from industrial farming to multi-crop sustainable farming and the federal government will help foot the bill for the switchover. Give your farm a mix of grains, vegetables, fruit trees, and animals to make it sustainable and environmentally friendly, and the government will be there to help you during the transition. In addition to the cash bribes, the government will also offer programs and consultants to teach farmers how best to use their land sustainably.

On the flip side, if any farm chooses not to go this route, all farming subsidies end. No more artificially inflated prices for industrial crops, no tax breaks for growing or breeding them, all of it, gone. If you choose to try and put profit ahead of the environment, you're going to do it without the help of the government to do so.

In addition to growing food products, I'm going to add a new requirement for all farms, whether they choose the deal or not. Going forward, all farms must allow for 10% of their land to be given over to growing hemp. We are going to be moving away from a tree based paper and petroleum based plastics to hemp and to do this, we're going to need hemp and a lot of it. Hemp is a useful weed that can grow almost anywhere and be harvested several times a year. Hemp can be made into paper, plastic, and fiber for clothing, just to name a few of the things it is useful for.

If we are going to have a sustainable society, hemp is one of the easiest ways to support the changeover, and change we will. Not only for us, but for all the future generations after us. We owe this to them, a healthy planet to live on where they do not struggle to breathe in the air, and starvation is not a way of life.

I realize this is a very small chapter considering the vast ramifications of what I am proposing. Feeding our people, correcting the damage done to our environment with industrial farming, and converting the way we approach farming is a lot of changes. I also know this is not something I can plan on my own, which is why I simply proposed some of the solutions I feel we need to make to correct these problems. But, I know we have experts out there, and even existing agencies within our government who can help flesh out what I have proposed into workable plans. We're counting on you guys to step up and help us, and maybe even take a few more steps ahead than I did and create something truly grand. Now is your chance to be the hero I know you have always secretly dreamed of being.

Ooooah... another blank page to doodle on!

CHAPTER EIGHT
ENERGY

Energy, we need it to sustain the societies we have built. The question is, where are we going to get it from? We have to be reasonable here and acknowledge digging fuel out of the ground is neither efficient or cost effective, nor is it good for anything living on this planet.

But that's okay, because we are an innovating species and we are already working on the solutions for our problems. All we have to do now is put them to use rather than gathering dust while dying industries block their implementation, all in the name of profit.

This is a subject I know bits and pieces about, but the nitty-gritty application of integrating multiple renewable energy sources into a cohesive system, you guessed it, I'm gonna need your help. But, for now, let's go over some general things that will help and other things we can do while I wait for a report from my faithful followers in green and sustainable tech.

Unlike many of the other chapters, this one is quite small considering the vast ramifications of what I am proposing. But, as I said, this is not an area I am an expert in, I have a vision of a clean future, what I need now from you is the know-how to make the system work.

We are going to break away from our dependence on oil, gas and nuclear power. We have the tech, now we apply the will, together.

Also, I'm getting rid of Daylights Savings Time!

SOLAR & WIND

Let's start with some basics, solar. This will probably be the backbone of our new energy grid. Not only in the form of solar farms, which will be important, but in homes all across America. Over time, every home in America will be equipped with solar roof tiles and become part of our nation's energy grid. Advances are being made all the time in researching solar, and one of the best new ones I've seen is solar roof tiles, made to look like shingles and installed in a similar manner.

So, going forward, all new home construction will have roofs made of solar shingles (provided something better doesn't come along, but we're going with this right now because it's what we have). All standard tar and asphalt shingles will be phased out completely during the changeover. Grants and low-interest loans can be applied for if your company makes shingles and you would like to be part of the future making solar shingles.

As older homes need roof repairs, they will be replaced with the newer solar shingles and help will be given by local electric companies to install the necessary inverters to complete the process.

Solar roads will also be looked into. The tech for them shows a great deal of promise, and if that promise turns out to be a workable solution, it will be implemented as fast as they can make the tiles. For those not familiar with solar roads, a small tech company has come up with the idea of hexagon solar road panels to replace existing road construction materials.

There are additional bonuses that come with this tech outside of generating energy. Such as, helping to keep the roads clear of ice and snow because of the heat they generate. They use LED lights so at night the road lines clearly show up to light our way, and can be changed as conditions change, such as altering turning lanes or redirecting traffic after an accident. And, if a tile goes bad, instead of tearing up an entire section of road, you simply pop up the broken tile and snap in its replacement. The roads can be used to power not only our homes and businesses, but our vehicles, by adding charging stations along our roadways to lower our dependence on oil even further.

In this country, we have vast areas of desert, some of which is used as farmland and using copious amounts of limited water supplies to irrigate fields. We need to end these practices.

But, I also understand the plight of the farmers working those areas not wanting to lose their livelihood. To that end, I propose a partnership initiative to lease those lands to turn them into solar arrays, or wind farms, depending on which would work best in that area. Farmers who wish to learn the daily operations of this new venture will be given free education to become the foreman of each of these farms and put in charge of the daily operations. If they choose this option, they will be paid not only for the use of their land but given a percentage of the profits each quarter. If they do not, then they will be given two options, they can continue to live on the property and be given a quarterly rent, or they can sell the property outright to the government and move on to find greener pastures.

Wind generators are another part of this equation and new strides are being made every day. From giant turbines that soar into the sky to small ones that can be put on rooftops, wind is everywhere, a renewable resource only waiting to be harnessed. Some are being made to do more than capture the wind and turn it into energy, but used to lower carbon emissions and clean the air of pollutants as well. We need to integrate both of these concepts into our power system. I have seen designs that are not only efficient but aesthetically pleasing to the eye and can be added to our cities without a cry of alarm from residents. The goal is to seamlessly integrate these systems into our daily living in a way that residents look forward to their construction waiting to see what new marvel they will behold when it is done.

Dams have been a part of our energy grid for a while now, but I have mixed feeling about them. Their construction and continued use can cause catastrophic ecosystem collapses as we stockpile water for our use. I don't intend to start tearing them down, but I also do not wish to encourage continued construction of them unless it can be shown to create an overall net positive result, not just for people, but for the wildlife surrounding those areas. For this, I will rely on experts who can judge this type of construction better than I would ever be able to do.

This isn't to say this is a complete list of what we should do to help change how we produce power for our nation. We will be using solar, wind, and water to power our world and we will get better at it as we continue to invest money in these products. There are strides forward in turning everyday items like house siding and paint into power producers and new, fanciful wind generators that not only produce energy but are pleasing to the eye.

The more we invest, the better our returns will be in this industry. I plan on investing heavily in our future and when we are done, our country will become a marvel of green tech for the world to behold.

A DYING INDUSTRY

Like the dinosaur, the era of oil, gas, and coal is coming to an end. And while it is good for us collectively, for those losing their jobs in these areas, it can seem like the end of the world. Okay, first, take a deep breath, and now relax. This isn't the end of the world, it's the beginning of a new one, a better one for you and your children (if you have any). But, like all new beginnings, it can be scary and a bit bumpy, but as your caring Dictator, I want to make this transition as smooth as possible.

To begin, even as those old jobs fall away, new jobs are being created and you can be a part of that if you choose to be. If you do, (and we are really going to need your help in this) I will be implementing training programs for all the areas we are working on becoming a new way of life in our country. We are going to need construction workers, electricians, manufacturers, an entire workforce dedicated to nothing more than changing our energy system from oil, gas, and coal to the new system of renewable energy.

During your training, you will be paid, comparable to what you were making prior to your job becoming obsolete. When your training is complete, we will match you to a job you are now qualified for. Because our entire country will be under construction for a while (please pardon our mess) relocation should not play a significant role in your opportunities for employment, but will be offered as an option.

In some cases, job training will not be necessary depending on the type of job. Some skill sets will be transferable, and in those cases, we will work to get you into one of these fields as quickly as possible.

To coordinate this, local unemployment offices will be used to match people to jobs. Pretty much as they have been doing since their inception. What will be new is the funding we will be adding to adequately provide resources, training, and employment support. Employment offices are often held in the same regards as a waiting room in hell, full of paper shuffling, scarce resources, and inadequate funding, resulting in long lines terminating in disappointment for the people who venture into them.

Now, they will be the starting point for a new venture in life for those who walk in the door. Intake interviews will be given to pinpoint a person's skills, aptitudes, and educational levels, and then design an individual program to meet each applicant's needs. Each person will be assigned a caseworker who will guide them through the paperwork and smooth the transition so no one feels confused, overwhelmed or discouraged.

And, it won't just be for training in new green tech fields, but if an individual wishes to make a complete life change and begin an entirely new career, that too will be supported. While we need new workers in rebuilding our infrastructure, perhaps it was never your calling, and you've had dreams of becoming something else but didn't have the time, money or opportunity to pursue other options. Now is your time. This is your life, make the most of it.

One last thing. Working in many of these old industries, such as coal mining, has been hard on the health of those who worked in them. Particularly, older workers suffer from a variety of conditions that affect their ability to work, yet have suffered through anyway, simply because there was no other option if they wished to continue eating and keep a roof over their heads.

First, let me state, we will not abandon you. As a citizen of this country, you are valuable and will not be discarded. As we get the UBI rolling, you will always have the option of retiring and living out the rest of your life living off your UBI. Or, you can be trained in a less physically demanding field. Or, you can take this opportunity to explore new options by reviving old hobbies into a new business.

The world is changing, and we will all be required to change with it. Some of it will be scary, and some will come with bumps along the way as we learn to navigate our new reality. But change doesn't always mean tragic, no matter how intimidating it can seem at the beginning. It's a bright new world that each of us will have a part in, and I hope you will take this opportunity to find your place in it.

THE GRID

We will be getting more into the power grid later in *Infrastructure*, but I did want to touch on a few points here. (There really is a lot of back and forth in all these chapters, isn't there? I'm doing my best to keep things organized, but the world is messy and hates being confined, even on paper.)

When it comes to alternative energy, integrated networking is the key. It's not about creating large systems, but combining millions of connections over vast areas to decentralize our power grid so if one area goes down, it doesn't cause rolling blackouts elsewhere in the system.

Our energy grid currently has a D- rating, and folks, that's barely passing for something we are so dependent on. We can, and we will, do better. By encouraging every home to become its own small substation, we take unmanageable strain off the system in times of disaster. Individual areas and homes will be affected, but it won't take the whole system down as power is rerouted around the damaged areas and most homes (depending on if they were damaged during a disaster) can power at least part of its own needs to muddle through the worst of it as we go about fixing what went wrong.

We also need to address our power lines and substations as well. They are old, outdated, and often an eyesore few want to live around, and can you blame them? We need to replace this dying system and remove the overhead power lines that clutter our skies and are so susceptible to the whims of the weather. Because we have all seen the devastation created in our communities in the wake of natural disasters with homes, lives, and livelihoods lost by the indifference of mother nature rolling over our country.

We need to start preparing ourselves for what is to come as climate change continues to flex the power of its new normal. Pretending climate change isn't real will not save us, but we can do more to keep the damage to a minimum when it does. Because the sad fact is, even if we all jump on to green tech train full force, it is still going to take at least a decade to correct what we have done to ourselves. And until then, the best we can do as we help the earth heal itself is build communities that are designed to cope with the weather in their area effectively.

Again, this is not an area I am an expert in. But there are experts out there and I will need you to step forward to help fix our electrical grid. We are all depending on you, so no pressure or anything, but none of us want to go back to living in the dark, and we will all be looking at you for help.

CHAPTER NINE
INFRASTRUCTURE

I hate to tell you this my fellow revolutionaries, but our country is falling apart at the seams, and slumlords are deciding what needs repair. There is no way we can continue to compete globally if everything, from roads to our internet, is falling into ruin and disrepair. Our highways used to be the shining standard of the world, now you can't travel anywhere without running into questionable bridges, potholes, and long stretches of road covered by orange barrels but no activity by even a single construction worker in sight.

Our sewer systems, more than anywhere, is where you can see the economic failures of widening income inequity. In an affluent area, even if it's considered "rural", would never go without something as basic as human waste removal. Yet, there are areas in our country that have no access to a septic tank, much less a sewer system. Human waste is literally being flushed out into their yards, if they're lucky, it might go into a shallow ditch, if they are not, it goes directly out to the topsoil of their yard. In an affluent neighborhood, a solution would be found to correct the situation. In a poor one, the residents simply have to deal with the hand they are given.

And in poor urban areas, the situation is not much better. You only have to look at Flint, MI to see the difference. The city decided to "save" a few pennies and allowed tainted water to be piped into the homes of people they considered less important. As part of the austerity measures the city decided to use after declaring a financial emergency, safe water was seen as less important than saving money. And, of course, once the actual damage was done, and people suffered and children were permanently damaged, the city reversed its decision, issued an apology and a health emergency was declared. But, it was too late for all those hurt in this decision.

This is something that would be undreamed of in an affluent area. It simply wouldn't happen. But sadly, it is happening to the most vulnerable among us, and continues on, disaster after disaster. Well, it ends now, with this administration. A person's worth should not be decided by the size of their bank account, and no human should ever be considered less valuable because of the job they have or where they live.

We are going to begin investing heavily in our infrastructure, and with those investments will come money and new opportunities for everyone. You gotta spend money to make money, and that doesn't just apply to the rich or to Wall Street, but everywhere. And our country is going to start spending money on infrastructure like a drunk sailor on leave.

Don't panic my friends as I talk about throwing more money at a problem because we will recoup most of the money we spend in one way or another. With every road built and sewer system upgraded it will mean jobs, new industries, opportunities for both individuals and big corporations and bring new interest to areas long thought lost. Our infrastructure has fallen into such a state of disrepair I could randomly throw a dart at a map and probably hit something that needs fixing, but we're going to be a bit more organized about it in our planning. Although, it would be kinda funny to base our repairs on a dartboard map... but we won't, (nope, nope, nope, giggle) no matter how amusing it would be!

Instead, we are going to target low-income areas and put them on the top of the list for repairs, moving up the social strata as we finish each project. At the end of my six years as your wonderful Dictator, my plan is to have every area of human habitation in our country brought up to an acceptable standard of living. Construction takes time, and it will have to continue after I am gone, but we can begin this together and once begun, it will be difficult to stop, even if the next leader of the free world doesn't share my enthusiasm for bringing the whole of our nation up to at least a basic standard of living.

And be prepared for the next round of screaming as we begin this. The privileged of our nation have become accustomed to always being at the head of the line for everything, and to be put lower on the list is probably going to upset some of them. But, after a few years, it is my hope they will finally see the wisdom of our actions and realize it helps them as well. Never underestimate the power of healthy self-interest, it might take them a bit to come around, but most will in time.

As I mentioned in the introduction of this chapter, the roads and bridges in our country are in a sad state of disrepair. Many of our bridges are being held up mostly by hopes and dreams that are frequently dashed when they collapse. Our roads are in desperate need of repairs, (from my years of travel throughout this country, I can report most of Indiana is under repair so much the official state motto should be changed to "Pardon our Mess"), and yet, overall, the roads don't seem to be improved despite all the orange barrels littering our highways.

As we talked about in *Energy*, solar roads (provided they prove their viability) will soon start replacing all of our roadways. Starting in areas currently slated for repairs, then moving outward from there. In places solar roadways are found not to be a practical solution, we will turn to other innovative technology, such as self-repairing concrete or recycled plastic.

Again, I will be looking for experts and innovators to step up and help organize this massive project that will span our nation. This will not be a simple job, and there will be many problems associated with our construction sites, because there are always problems with big projects. But difficult doesn't mean impossible, they just need to addressed and reasonable solutions found each time it happens.

Our bridges also need to be repaired or upgraded, and in many ways, it may be more important for us to fix them first before starting on our roads. If a road on a flat surface fails, it can be inconvenient (provided it's not a gaping sinkhole), but if a bridge fails, it can be deadly. So, we will prioritize our repairs based not on the affluence of an area, but on how deadly the failing structure is.

As part of these upgrades, I would also like to see new additions such as animal crossing bridges added to high risk areas along migration routes. And, as each section is completed, all environmental damage that may have occurred with our construction will be repaired as a standard part of any construction site.

Each state will be required to submit a full report of each of their roadways and bridges, listing them in order of risk of failure. Those lists will be submitted to the Federal Highway Commission within six months of my assuming office, and funding secured within a reasonable timeframe to ensure all the upgrades needed are addressed for each state. Our interstate systems will be restored and we'll bring our nation up to the standards we held to not so long ago in our past.

WATER & SEWER

Many of our water and sewer systems are a sad mess. We have places that haven't seen upgrades in over a hundred years, and honestly, that's scary. Plumbing is what defines civilization going back beyond the Roman Empire. The ability to bring water to people in their homes and carry out our waste is central to the functioning of any area inhabited by people. To put it bluntly, if water failed to come in and waste pooled in the streets because it couldn't get out, New York City would be uninhabitable in a matter of days. And yet, NYC has some of the oldest pipelines in use in our country. I don't know about you, but I'd want to be anywhere but New York if the sewers failed.

Although I am not an expert in pipelines, I do understand there are many difficulties associated with upgrading older systems, particularly in high population areas. But difficult doesn't mean impossible, and bluntly, must be done if our cities are to remain safely habitable.

We will also be addressing rural areas that do not have any kind of sewer system at all to serve their population. These areas are unsafe and create bio-hazards that bring the possibility of parasites and water born diseases which are detrimental to the people living there. If you were unaware of this, ringworm, a parasite found almost exclusively in third world nations, has made a resurgence in our country. That's how bad it's gotten.

Are you beginning to feel a little overwhelmed by everything we have to fix in our nation? Yeah, me too. But still, all of this needs to be done unless we are content to slide into being a third-world nation, despite all our wealth and potential. And I, for one, am not content to let that happen. We still have several more chapters to go, and the list of repairs keeps growing with every page, but we have neglected our repairs for so long our country is on the verge of collapse and now we're gonna have to address a decade of neglect in less than six years. So... take a deep breath before we go on. It's okay, I understand...

Now, back to repairing our sewers and water lines. Before too much longer, it's going to seem like most of our nation is going to be hanging a *pardon our mess* sign over every road, bridge, city and rural area, everywhere. And it won't be too far from the truth, but it is my hope, by coordinating most of these repairs we can keep our nation mobile while we install all the necessary upgrades without causing too much disruption. But, there will be delays, there will be disruption, and from time to time, minor inconveniences as repairs take some system offline for a time.

I will promise you this, the inconveniences will be worth it at the end. Safe water, reliable waste systems, a stable energy grid, better travel conditions, faster internet, reductions in disease and illnesses, and a healthier population will be our rewards for all our hard work. We are doing this, not just for ourselves, but for our children to grow up in a world that isn't falling into ruin.

So, my dear experts, it's time for you to step up and bring me a plan to fix all of this. I have given you an outline of what I see wrong with our current level of plumbing, it is up to you to create a workable plan for fixing it.

PLANES, TRAINS & AUTOMOBILES

My fellow compatriots, we need to face the fact that our trains are pathetic. Everywhere else in the world you can witness the magnificence of bullet trains and mag rails, while we chug along in Thomas the Train sets. We can do better people.

Affordable mass transit is central to a well functioning society. Our ability to send goods and people from Point A to Point B and have it be reliable, affordable and with reasonable travel time is important to both business and people. We haven't invested in our railways anywhere near what is needed to keep us competitive with the rest of the world, and I'm pretty sure they snicker behind our backs and say things like "how quaint" when talking about our transit systems. The technology is there, being used by every other country in the world, we simply haven't embraced it. We will now give that tech a great big hug and start upgrading our railways.

This is again another problem we will need to throw money at to fix. And, yes, I know, I'm throwing a lot of money around to fix these problems, but you can either fix something or let it fall down, and I'm not willing to let our country fall down because of a lack of upkeep.

I would like to see proposals on my desk within six months on how to begin upgrading our railways without causing excessive disruption to our current system. We need to keep the trains running on time, or at least to the best of our ability to do so, while construction is underway. In the end, I want our railways to be the jewels of our nation's transportation system, making them cost effective, and affordable, for those who wish to travel our nation without leaving the ground.

Our airports (personally, I hate airports, it's like visiting a despotic regime where all your rights are null & void while you visit) are in need of upgrades. Specifically, our air traffic control computers are in need of updating. We should also do something about the way we run our airports as well. I love to travel, but I'd rather pull my fingernails out with pliers than travel by plane anymore, not because I hate flying, but because I hate airports.

The last time I traveled by plane, after ransacking my carry-on and taking my toothpaste (because it was 0.5 ounces over the allowed amount), then making me partially undress because they thought my sweater was too bulky, I had to bite my tongue to keep from being put on the "no-fly" list for being snarky. I have refused to enter an airport since. Safety is important, turning our airports into dictatorships (not nearly as benign as mine) is an over-the-top reaction. To quote, "*Those who would give up essential Liberty, to purchase a **little** temporary Safety, deserve neither Liberty nor Safety.*" And that's exactly what we have done at our airports.

The knee-jerk reactions we have had since 9/11 have often skewed our perception of what constitutes a threat and what can safely be ignored. I agree we do need to protect ourselves, but our over-the-top reactions need to end. Our country right now is acting like an abuse victim, where every move is seen as a threat, even when it is not. It does not make us stronger, it makes us more vulnerable as we suffer from what is essentially PTSD on a nationwide scale. We were hurt, I understand that pain, I watched the Twin Towers fall as I cradled my newborn in my arms. I felt your fear and wondered what was going to happen next. But, it was our Congress who put true fear into my heart as I witnessed our representatives give into fear and lash out blindly because of fear. We waged a war because of fear. We have torn down entire nations because of fear. We have turned our public transit systems into oppressive regimes because of fear. And it is time to acknowledge our fear and face it head on with clear eyes, no longer blindly lashing out, thinking any reaction, no matter how out of proportion, is better than nothing.

So, I want a full review of all of our policies and begin to scale down our over-the-top reactions and bring some sanity back into our responses. We will also be reviewing our no-fly list policy. Presently, there is no way to be removed once you are on it, even if you were put on the list by mistake. I also wish to see a full list of what we need to bring all of our airport systems up to date to stay competitive with the rest of the world. We can do this my friends, we can go forward without letting fear dictate our responses and still keep ourselves safe.

And lastly, automobiles. Gasoline engines are soon going to go the way of the horse & buggy, and like it or not, it will happen, it is now up to us to be prepared for that future. We can try to fight it like horse owners of old once did, yelling at cars that passed "*Get a*

IF I WERE DICTATOR

horse!" but it didn't end well for them, and it won't end well with us.

Tesla is currently leading the charge for electric engines. Of course, they are out of reach for many in our country right now. Then again, before Ford, the automobile was thought of the same way. Like all other technology, the more we buy, the cheaper and more accessible it gets. To bring this tech to the people, I want our government to start investing more in R & D into alternatives to combustion engines that are affordable, sustainable, and accessible. Perhaps look into cash incentive programs to encourage people to invest in purchasing existing alternate vehicles. Or publicly subsidize manufacturers to drive down the cost.

However we decide to address this, one way or another, we will need to invest, both as individuals and as a country going forward.

INTEGRATING OUR SYSTEMS

Throughout this book, I have hit on the common theme of decentralizing our energy grid and bringing in more renewable tech to move us out from under gas, oil, and coal. To do this, I have proposed everything from individually powered solar homes to government owned solar highways and wind farms, and everything in between. I am also open to more suggestions on other ways to shift us off our dirty energy habit because every little bit helps.

But with all these new systems going online, we are going to have to rework how our grid operates and get everyone integrated into the new system. The how's of it, I am going to leave to the experts, they will undoubtedly know much better than I, how to make this work.

My goal is to make our country an abundant clean energy producer that everyone can benefit from. The more power we create, the cheaper it will become and those savings will spread out to every individual, saving them upwards of thousands of dollars every year. The current power providers may find themselves in a bad spot because of all of this, and will probably join the screaming of other corporations I have upset throughout this book. They can join the chorus, but if we are committed to our revolution, they cannot stop us.

There are some things that are best left to profit driven companies, others, like our basic systems, are not. When water and power come under the purview of profit driven motivation, prices will always go up to meet shareholders expectations, leaving what is best for people near the bottom of the list of their priorities. So, we will begin to buy back our electric companies and they will become public ownerships, instead of private. Each state will be in charge of what their state produces, and profits will be used for needed updates and upkeep. If additional federal funding is needed for critical upgrades, those will be provided to each state if requested. If those funds are needed, each state will have to submit a formal request, and provide funding information, what their current proceeds are going to, and how much they can commit to the project.

This will also apply to any water or sewer treatment facilities that have been sold away from city municipalities. Those will be purchased and brought under the control of each city once more. Each state will require all the municipalities in their state to provide a full report on the state of their water and sewer treatment facilities, what problems each has, and the cost of repairs. Clean water is essential to life, and our most precious resource.

Along with all of these changes, there will be changes to corporations buying water rights. The current situation is not acceptable, with companies buying large amounts of water for pennies and charging residents much higher rates for use. In areas hit by drought, allowing companies to continue siphoning off water for profit is abhorrently detrimental. The era of profits before people has come to an end with our revolution. They may scream and point to lower profit margins and demand things go back to the way it was when they made all the rules and the rest had to suffer for it, but we can listen to them scream and continue to do what we know is right, regardless of how mad it makes them.

I'm sure some of you are asking right now, will this cost a lot of money? Well, yes, as a matter of fact, it will. But, most of the losses will be recouped in the years to come, and whatever the cost, it is worth it to have clean water and air. You can't drink money or breathe wealth and hope to survive. There are times when cost becomes the secondary consideration, and this is one of them.

Our country currently has some of the slowest internet in the world, *and* we pay more for the privilege. Monopolies have squeezed us for all the traffic would bear, while providing the least amount of speed or reliability compared to just about anywhere else in the world. Even our high-speed cable internet is sluggishly slow compared to other countries. We simply haven't kept up. And most of those companies are still using the network cables our government supplies as the backbone of their internet with little motivation to upgrade. Because these companies know, as long as people need the internet they'll take slow speed over no speed if it's their only option.

In this modern world, it is almost impossible to do anything without the internet. It's how we pay our bills, listen to music, talk with friends, apply for jobs, look up information and so much more. Even still, there are areas in our country with limited, or no access to internet of any kind, and those communities suffer for their lack. To make matters worse, when municipalities have stepped up to provide internet to their communities, they have run into power blocks by internet & phone companies demanding they stop, because it interferes with their potential profits (sigh, with an eye-roll). I plan on changing that.

We have allowed our internet to come under the hostile embrace of monopolies who feel no need to upgrade or provide decent service because they know the people have nowhere else to go but to them. People are trapped with limited choices and all the providers set similar prices and speeds, so it doesn't matter where they go, they are ultimately going to be in the same spot whichever company they choose to go with.

So, to combat this problem, we will begin to create internet access through municipalities in each community, working in conjunction with state and federal oversight to bring our internet up to the standards of the rest of the world. Current companies who offer internet are allowed to continue as they are, but they are no longer allowed to offer resistance to municipal owned internet. If they want to keep their customers, they are going to have to step up and upgrade, and set reasonable prices, to remain competitive. If they are unwilling to do so, they can stop providing internet services as part of their packages.

At the end of my term, I will see to it that every area in our country, urban or rural, has affordable, dependable, and fast internet. If we are to stay competitive as a country, this is something we must do.

How you doing? Take a few deep breaths if you need to.

CHAPTER TEN
THE MILITARY

Before we begin this, let me state for the record, I am not going to bash our soldiers. I was a military wife for 13 years and saw my (then) husband through two deployments and experienced the heartache and hardship of deployment. I have a great deal of respect for our soldiers, each and every one of them, and they deserve our best, and I don't mean rhetorically, but in tangible practice. So, take my word for it, the military is something I know a little bit about.

Now that we have gotten that out of the way, we need to talk about the bloating of our military funding. And even with all the bloat, only small slivers of funding creep down to our actual military force. Most of the budget goes towards contracts, civilian contractors, and honestly, a whole lot of waste no one knows where it went to. One of the last audits of the Pentagon it was discovered 6.5 trillion dollars, (yeah, you read that right, trillion, with a T) was completely unaccounted for. Money had come in, cash had gone out, but not one single person could say where it disappeared to. Just gone. Poof. Somehow they misplaced 6.5 trillion dollars.

That my friend is a lot of money to misplace. I'm a little panicky if I misplace twenty dollars, I'd probably die of heart failure if I found out I misplaced a trillion dollars, much less 6.5 of them. Good lord that's a lot of money! Okay... I'll give you all a minute to process this and get over the cold shakes over the loss of so much cash.

When you're ready, flip over to the next page. Take as much time as you need... it's okay, I understand.

MILITARY CONTRACTS

Better now? Are you ready to continue? If not, take a few more deep breaths and let's slog on with this. That 6.5 trillion is gone and there's no getting it back, and honestly, probably not worth the effort to try. The money went down the rabbit hole and will never be seen again. Sadly wave it goodbye... now, onward!

If the military can misplace that kind of cash and not even notice, I think it's a good indicator we are giving them way too much money. That being said, there are things we need to spend money on, but we have got to be better about how we allot the military budget.

To begin, let's start with military contracts. Analysts have estimated the military spends around $7 billion a year on things they neither want, nor need. Like tanks. Like aircraft frames for planes we no longer fly. Like replacement parts for vehicles no longer in use. Like buying 100 of an item when only 2 are needed. And it all adds up, fast.

Some of this is because we have contracts with a company, and want it or not, we have been obligated to continue buying the item anyway. So they are bought, dumped on the military to deal with, some poor supply officer sighs, shake their head and find another location to store whatever was bought, never to see the light of day again. It's a waste of time, material, space, and most of all, money.

So, effective immediately, as your fiscally responsible Dictator, I am halting all military contracts until a full review can be done and proof provided, whatever is being purchased is actually needed. And, if it turns out we don't need it, we are not going to buy it, so please stop making them. Seriously, just stop. We're not going to buy your junk anymore because of a piece of paper. There has got to be some common sense to this and you're just going to have to deal. After taking advantage of all of us for years in your pursuit of profits with unnecessary purchases shoved down our throats, it's going to stop.

I am also halting all payout to companies we have contracts with who have promised something, but hasn't as of yet, delivered. Which is another rampant problem when it comes to military spending. A company says, I'll make X for you, and it will be ready by Y time. The military says, sounds great, here's a basketful of money for it! Then Y time comes, and X isn't delivered. Production delays, performance delays, it was a stupid idea, but we sold it anyway, delays. We're still paying for it, but it never actually arrives on time or as promised. It's a problem. And one we can simply solve. If X doesn't arrive by Y time, you are not going to get paid. No more pre-payments, you get the money when we get the item.

Now, onward to civilian contractors. Yeah, about 90% of you have got to go. Take this as part of your termination of contract notification. I am going tell you something anyone in the military will affirm, civilian contractors hurt morale. If it's a job that can be done by a soldier, it should be done by a soldier, from cook to computer tech. And there was a time in our not too distant past where all those jobs were filled by soldiers and only an occasional specialist brought in when it was deemed necessary but too costly to train a soldier for such a specialized job.
During the Bush era, this started to change and more civilian contractors were brought in to do the jobs of soldiers, generally at 4 times the pay and with none of the restrictions imposed by the military code of conduct. Can you imagine being an E3 army truck driver, working beside a civilian contractor, doing the exact same job and you're paid $22,000 a year and they're paid $80,000 (or more)? Yeah, it pisses them off and causes a great deal of grumbling among our soldiers, and rightly so.
I will give the military a year to shift training and fill the slot openings caused by vacating civilian contractors. At the end of the year, if the military needs a job to be done, they will need to supply their own. If it is a highly specialized job that isn't frequently used and not cost effective to train a soldier to do the job, an exemption can be made, but every request for an exemption will be carefully investigated first.
During the switchover year, all civilian contracts will be reduced in pay to match the corresponding military pay for whatever job they are contracted for. Sorry, but fair is fair.

With that done, I'm pretty sure we've freed up at least a couple billion dollars. So, what are we going to do with all that money? Don't worry, I have ideas...

OUR SOLDIERS

I'm sorry to say, now that I'm going to make healthcare and education universal, getting people to join the military may become more problematic, since those are two of the most often quoted reasons for joining. Followed closely by, lack of options and don't want to starve. Which, with the improvement to a living wage, training programs, college and trade education, and UBI, joining the military is going to be a hard sell.

Now don't get me wrong, there are people out there for personal or family tradition reasons wish to join the military, and I, as your beloved Dictator, salute you for it. But speaking confidentially just between you and me, we both know there's not enough of you to fill out the ranks.

So, to start with, we're going to increase your pay. How much, you ask with a smile. Truthfully, I have no idea... yet. Military calculations are different than civilian pay equivalents. Even though we took away healthcare and education as part of the incentive, there is still housing allowance if you live off base, separate rats, dependents allowance, travel allowances, free food at the chow line, and full retirement at the end of 20 years in addition to the UBI. So, those remain, and they are nice, but is it enough to make you want to risk life and limb in service to your country? Probably not by themselves. So, you're going to receive a pay raise, but I'm going to need help with the calculations from people smarter than me when it comes to selecting the wage allotments for all ranks, plus time served, job specialty, etc. to make it fair and appealing.

But, to ballpark it, we'll start with, you'll receive the equivalent of slightly above minimum wage during training, plus, of course, free housing, food, dependents allowance (if applicable) and all the free training you could ask for. After finishing training and you become a full soldier, you'll get a raise. Most likely pay grades will be scaled, but what the scale will be is something we'll need to work out. But, I will take care you. You will also be receiving your UBI, joining the military will not change that.

There will be other incentives, like sign on bonuses, reenlistment bonuses, and other types of bonuses to be sprinkled on your throughout your career, and it is my hope when you join, it is for the purpose of making the military a career for your full 20. I want to encourage people when joining to make a career out of it, not just short jaunts through the military as is often the case now. We need experienced soldiers who can give balance to all the young ones coming in and to ensure our military is the finest military force in the world. Dedicated men and women who hold the ideal of keeping our country safe and secure as your heart's priority are the people we need in uniform.

As part of your package deal, there will be housing. And this I will promise you, they will be nice and they will be well cared for, whether it is in family housing or individual soldier apartments. As part of housing, utilities such as electric, water, and internet will be included, and just because I love you all so much, I'm going to throw in a standard cable package. Am I starting to sweeten the deal enough for you to start thinking, maybe the military might be for me?

Continuing education will, of course, be a part of the package. Keeping our soldiers trained and competitive is important not only to our soldiers individually, but for our country collectively. I want each of you not only to know which way to point a gun, but to be well-versed in languages, other cultures, and diplomacy, if you have an inclination for it. Our military will have the best tech to play with, and all the training that goes with it, and even learn about the civilian applications, so if after your 20 years are done, your skills will be sought after in the civilian world. And when you retire, if you simply want to enjoy the rest of your life, you will continue to be cared for by the military with a generous retirement plan in addition to your UBI.

And, if something were to happen to you during your career, whether it was war related or you fell down a flight of stairs, your family will be taken of. Your spouse or designated survivor would be provided for, and your children cared for and supported until they reach adulthood. Your family can remain on base if they choose to do so, or receive help in relocation, if not. Additional services will be provided to your family as they deal with your loss as needed. The military takes care of its own.

For those who have served through the many wars the U.S. has been engaged in, we can do better for you as well. Mental health services will be a priority. The suicide rates are far too high, and the lives devastated by war far too costly, for things to continue as they are. For those of you who have been injured in the line of duty, you have my solemn promise that you will receive the best medical care available, and will make sure that your housing accommodates your disability. If you are a homeless vet, please go to your nearest recruiting station and, to begin with, temporary housing will be found for you. For the long term, as my time as your Dictator progresses, I will be making housing for all a reality and that will absolutely include you. Your service to your country will not go unnoticed or without reciprocation. For those of you who have lost a spouse, a parent or a child, my heart goes out to each and every one of you, and we will take care of you as well. Nothing will bring back your loved one, but your sacrifice will not go unnoticed. It may be a bit shaky at first as we hit the ground, but all of these things will be a priority in our country going forward.

Along with everything else that will go into revamping our military, I will also give you this promise. I will never send you off to war without a clear and compelling reason. I will never put you into harm's way thoughtlessly nor without careful consideration and exhaustion of all other options first. I value each and every one of you and I will not squander your love or commitment to the safety of our country. And, as those who know me will attest, I do not go back on a promise made, whatever the personal cost to keeping it might be. You have placed your lives in my hands, and I do not take that lightly and it is with great reverence that I say, thank you for your trust in me.

So, we'll work together to make your service to our country worth your while and together we will help keep our nation strong, cradled in your capable hands. I welcome your suggestions, sent up through the chain of command, to build a strong, healthy, and respected military not only at home, but abroad.

A CALL TO WAR

As of late, our country has entered into several wars, countless skirmishes, dropped bombs on people without a declaration of war, and in general, have thrown our military might around like a bully kicking sand at the scrawny kid on the beach. I'm sorry my friends, but we cannot continue to do this. It's not good for us, and it's certainly not good for the people we are dropping bombs on.

We are not making friends wherever we go, and looking back at history, we haven't had the best track record when it comes to our interference. The sad fact is, we've done as much damage as any help we may have given, and the rest of the world isn't thanking us for our efforts as they try to dig themselves out from under the rubble we caused.

The war on terrorism isn't working. We are no better off, or safer, than we were when we first declared war on it. It's worked out about as well as our war on alcohol when we created Prohibition. Not very.

I'm going to share with you the best advice those familiar with terrorism will tell you. You cannot bomb terrorism out of existence, you only make more terrorists that way. *So, what are we supposed to do*, you are now demanding I'm sure. You're not going to like the answer, but I'll give it to you anyway. Nothing. Yes, you heard me, nothing. We don't go after them, we don't engage with them outside of imminent threat, we don't bomb them, we don't give their neighbor's guns, we don't train their enemies, we simply do, nothing.

Yeah, that's a hard pill to swallow, but the truth often is.

Every time we bomb a town, the odds are at least some of those left alive who never before considered becoming a terrorist will now run, as soon as they are able, to their local terrorist recruiting location. Why? Well, let me ask you this. If some country dropped a bomb on your hometown because they didn't like something our country was doing in the world and killed your friends, maybe a family member, or your child, would you shrug your shoulders and say, "oh, yeah, my country did something bad so we deserved this" or would you drop everything and run to your nearest recruiting station wanting to dispense some payback? (9/11 ringing any bells for you?) Yeah, we both know the answer, and it wouldn't be shrugging your shoulders and going on with your life. We have been creating far more terrorists with our actions than we will ever eliminate, and so the answer is, we stop.

We address specific, credible threats to our nation and to our populations, but we will not be taking the fight to them anymore. Nor will we be providing any arms, ammunition, or equipment to any other nation for any reason. We are going to be scaling back our military industrial complex, and the government will no longer be the arms broker for the world.

We will begin to immediately scale back our overseas operations, from wars we are engaged in to military bases. And, unless it is a case of genocide or clear humanitarian crisis, we will not be taking sides in any conflict if it does not directly engage our country. Our military is there to protect us from outside threats, not to take on the world and force it to its knees.

Now, that being said, there may come a time when our nation must answer the call of war. When taking our soldiers outside our borders is in the best interest of the world, and not a knee-jerk reaction out of fear or greedy self-interest for resources. And, if that time ever comes, we will act.

But, we need to put safeguards in place to prevent the wanton warmongering we have lately been engaging in. During the time of the Roman Empire, wars were lead by their leaders or their firstborn sons, no conflict was entered into unless those who called for war had skin in the game. Perhaps it's not such a bad idea now. If the ruling body who decides war is to be called, but experiences no personal consequences for their decision, that body tends to make light of war, knowing the conflict will never reach their door.

Or, perhaps other, and better, safeguards can be found to keep our legislators well grounded in the consequences of war so they never attempt to involve our country without a clear and compelling reason. While I am dictator, this will never happen, but there will come a time in the not too distant future, it will not be in my hands, but of those of Congress, so we'd better put those guards in place before it's up to them.

I also believe there should be a public vote on whether or not we go to war. And, if the majority decides it is in our best interest, every person who voted yes will be at the top of the list of draftees if more soldiers are needed.

IF I WERE DICTATOR   149

Or perhaps, there could just be a random 10% assortment from anyone who voted yes to be picked for the war lottery, and it would include any member of our government who voted yes.

I'm open to suggestions on this. But I never again want to see a single soldier put into harm's way from a war waged over profits, foreign resources, or power for the sake of power.

Now, let go on to making friends...

There's two more chapters to go. Still with me?

CHAPTER ELEVEN
INTERNATIONAL RELATIONS

Alright everyone, we need friends. Our country cannot continue to bully the rest of the world and not expect to eventually be forced to pay for the consequences of our hubris. We need other countries to like us, not because we give them guns. Nor hate us because we use those guns against them. We, and I'm sorry if this upsets you hearing this, need to start behaving better.

We need to stop meddling in the personal affairs of other countries. We need to stop bombing countries. We need to stop engaging with terrorists. And we need to stop creating wars out of greed. Because honestly my friends, it hasn't worked out so great for anyone. Not for the lives lost among our soldiers, not for the lives lost among those we've gone to war with, and not for the trillion lost and countries left in ruin while waging wars across the globe.

Now, even though we are going to be scaling back our military operations, we will begin to advance humanitarian efforts, working closely with the U.N. as we do so. To begin, we will not step in unless we are asked, or in the case of genocide will give support providing humanitarian aid, and only with the majority support of other world nations for our interference. We will no longer be blundering along, making things worse and have the world hate us for our mistakes. Nor will we decide for other countries what is best for them, regardless of their wishes.

We will begin rebuilding our relationships with other nations and, most importantly, we will start listening to them. We are not always right, and have had the bad habit in the past to think we know more about what needs to be done than the country we are stomping around in. Rarely have we taken the time to understand the people or the culture before interfering, and then, when we get tired of stirring the pot, leave behind a mess that takes them generations to recover from after we packed up our toys and left. Instead of stabilizing other nations, we have destroyed them from the inside out, all with the best of intentions, of course, but the fact remains, we messed up and we've left them to clean up after us.

Going forward, we will work hand-in-hand with the United Nations to bring about stability. We will never again go it alone or use force and/or threats to make others fall in line with our demands. We're going to change from being big brother to best friend. An honest best friend, you know, that friend who always has your back, but is never afraid to call you out for bad behavior. Supportive, helpful and always listens to what you need, without making you feel bad about it. That's going to be us.

We are a strong nation, and the strong should always protect the weak, but there has to be a better way than what we have been doing up until now. And so, I propose, as your humble Dictator, the beginning steps in that direction, the Peacekeepers.

THE PEACEKEEPERS

The primary reason for war comes down to resources, who has them and who doesn't. Those who don't envy those that do, and when populations begin to starve and struggle, wars and revolutions erupt. As part of the effort to stem the tides of war, a new branch of the military will be created, The Peacekeepers. Their job will be to go into nations we have been invited to and help the local populations rebuild, replant, and return their lives to some semblance of normalcy. We will not go in and decide for them, instead (radical idea that this is), we will work with them to provide the things that are needed and necessary for a functioning society. The goal of the Peacekeepers is to help stabilize a country or an area by providing food, shelter, and security to the affected region until they can once again thrive on their own.

We will provide engineers, agriculture specialists, farmers, building contractors, and green tech specialists to help their local populations rebuild. We will help coordinate the building and staffing of schools, hospitals, and city centers. If a population has been devastated by famine, we will help feed the population until they can harvest their own crops and rebuild their livestock, or help invest in business infrastructure to build viable trade products. We will help train people for their public services, such as firefighters, police officers, paramedics, and public workers. We will not be there to take over those jobs, but to help train their populations to do those jobs for themselves.

At the beginning of this new dictate, each branch of the military will shift over a fourth of their personnel to these efforts. Bonuses will be given to any soldier who wishes to be trained, or already has a degree/training in a necessary field, and wishes to join the Peacekeepers. Each Peacekeeper will be trained in self-defense, but will use force only as a last resort to save your life or another. You get a sidearm and a combat knife, but no other weapons. Peacekeepers will be stationed with U.N. sanctioned forces who are charged with keeping the peace in the area. The job of a Peacekeeper isn't war, it's peace through humanitarian efforts. We are guests in their country, not an invasion force.

Every Peacekeeper mission will rest on these three principles, security, shelter, sustenance. The three basic things all human beings need to thrive in a society. We are not there to reform their culture, or impose our will upon them, but to help them learn to stand on their own again, so when we pack up we're no longer leaving behind a mess, but a functional society capable of caring for itself.

Before a Peacekeeper unit is called into action, there will be a clear and understood goal to their mission. As each unit's end goal is attained and their mission completed, they will leave the country and return to their home base. No Peacekeeper will ever be sent without a complete mission objective, with realistic and attainable goals to be met. They will never be sent on open ended missions or without a defined plan of action. If the goal is to build 50 solar arrays, then when 50 solar arrays are built, their mission is complete and they will go home.

But, because I know no plan survives first contact, Peacekeepers will the flexibility to modify their plan of action to accommodate unforeseen circumstances. But a Peacekeeper isn't a permanent solution to a temporary problem, they are there to help fix a specific situation, not become a crutch to lean on. Their goal is not only build something but to train the local population on how to maintain what they have built after they are gone. From agriculture to infrastructure, we want to build up a country from the inside out so they can stand independently, with pride, and continue on without help.

Caring for people can be expensive, but war costs even more. Ask any soldier what war has cost them and you will find the price was often much too high to be paid. Our nation has the biggest military budget in the world, spending more than the next ten countries combined. As with the shifting of military personnel, we will also be shifting over of military funding for this project. And yes, it will not be cheap, but then again, neither will it cost more than what we are already spending, in fact, I am willing to bet the returns on our investment in the future will be far greater than the returns we are currently getting for our war efforts.

For the world to work, for all of us, it must be stable. The job of a Peacekeeper to make that happen. It may be the most important task I'll ever ask of any of you, to help make the world a better place, not just for our country, but for the world we all live in. This is a task not just for our generation, but for all those who will come after us. We will plant trees we will never feel the shade of, for future generations to enjoy.

We have embassies all throughout the world. and as we scale back our military bases our embassies will take on a greater role throughout the world. With our new focus on friends, not bombs, the embassies will become central to building up our goodwill campaign. And yes, my friends, I am aware it's what an embassy is supposed to do, but sadly, that's not always what has happened in the past.

Before we go on, I want to be clear about a few things. I do not want our embassies to become military bases, but I do want them to become the central touchstone for deciding what kind of help we will be willing to offer to a host nation if asked. Please remember, we are guests, not the world's police, and many countries who will never need our help and our embassies will be mostly symbolic. Each embassy will be tailored to the country they are in, and the duties of our Ambassadors will reflect those differences. Ambassadors will be required to speak the language of the country they are assigned to, be familiar the local customs, and knowledgeable about its history. Unlike in the past, they will be experts in the host nation before they can be considered for an assignment.

It will be the Ambassador, with their staff, who will coordinate with both our country and the U.N. on topics related to stability and support as needed. Each embassy will have on staff experts in logistics, environmentalists, and other personnel necessary for the unique conditions of each country they are assigned to. This won't be a one size fits all situation, since each host nation will have its own particular issues and strengths, and every five years a review will be conducted to make sure their changing needs are addressed appropriately and modifications to staff needs are met. In cases of national disaster, it will be our embassy that will be responsible for reaching out to their host nation and coordinating services with local officials to help out in an emergency.

Each embassy will have a small contingent of soldiers stationed on the grounds for defense. But we will not be turning our embassies into substitutions for a military base in any country. The

IF I WERE DICTATOR 157

size of the force will be contingent on the general stability of the country they are in, and will also undergo five year evaluations same as the embassy support staff to address the changing needs of the nation they are in.

Our ambassadors will be the first line of contact between our nation and theirs. It will be to them that each country's officials will express any initial problems or concerns, and it will be the Ambassador's job to decide if this is something they can handle on their own, or if it needs to be addressed in a broader way by sending it up the chain of command back to Washington and possibly on to the U.N. if express action is needed.

An ambassador will also have the authority to contact their host nation if a problem is identified and, in their opinion, needs addressing may do so. If it is a humanitarian issue and the host nation does not share their concerns, the Ambassador can submit a report detailing their observations and what efforts were made to address them to the Foreign Affairs Office. If, after review, the Foreign Affairs Office agrees with the Ambassador's concerns, it will be handed over to Congress along with any other additional information they consider pertinent. If Congress agrees with the assessment, they will take their concerns to the U.N. and the world body will decide what will be the best course of action. Our nation will support the U.N. resolution addressing those concerns. Fully knowing, at times, the resolution may be to do nothing, and we will respect and honor those decisions, even if we don't agree.

If an agreement of action is granted, the Ambassador will be in charge of any Peacekeeper contingent assigned to the embassy and coordinate with the U.N., if necessary, about those arrangements. The embassy will also coordinate services and support between their host nation and the Peacekeepers job duties. But, before any Peacekeepers are assigned, the embassy will first submit their recommendations for what services and specialties will be needed to complete clearly defined goals. Once the requested personnel arrive, the embassy will assign them to their tasks and receive regular updates on their activities and supply the Peacekeepers with whatever is needed to complete their assignments. When each individual unit completes its mission, the embassy will arrange for the Peacekeeper unit to return home. Each Peacekeeper unit will have their own goals, timetable and mission assignments, and will be individually utilized and returned home as each finishes their assigned tasks.

The United States will no longer be "going it alone" and

imposing ourselves upon other nations without regard to the general world sentiment. We may be strong, but that doesn't always mean we are right, and we need to respect others if we are to be respected in return.

It is not in our best interest to become an isolationist nation, but neither do I wish for us to continue on our current course of deciding the fate of other nations without regard to their wishes. We need to be good neighbors to our fellow countries, which means we need to respect others as we wish to be respected. To hear their voices, and concerns, and respond with compassion when it is needed. If we can do those things, we can become the shining example our nation has always striven to be since the founding of our nation. I have faith in us, and I believe we can be that, and so much more, if we try to be a good neighbor rather than a cop.

SEEKERS

There are a great many things our country should be proud of, but, for many years we have been falling behind almost every other First World nation in terms of happiness, security, longevity, maternal mortality, education, healthcare, and innovation, just to name a few.

Throughout the world, other nations are pulling ahead of us in almost every area, for one reason or another, and have found new ways to address age-old problems. It's time for us to catch up, and with hope, exceed their standards. Every country has instituted various policies to address the problems their country faces, with varying degrees of success. To find out what those countries are doing differently, and figure out ways to apply their successful solutions to our problems, I am going to start a new program, the Seekers.

Seekers will not go into countries to talk to politicians, but to the people. We will be sending in a pair of historians and sociologists to every part of the world we are welcome to ask these 3 questions:

1. What do you like best about your country?
2. What do you like least?
3. If you could change one thing, what would it be?

Seekers will not interfere with local politics nor attend political events. Their job is to talk to ordinary citizens and find out what is working, and perhaps most importantly, what is not working in each nation. Each seeker pair will travel through the country, and stay at a new location every week before moving on. At the end of the week, each seeker will type up a report from that area to be added to their overall report at the end of six months.

If a seeker is asked why they are asking these questions, answer truthfully, we want to know what is working for you to help make our country better. This is not going to a secret, nor will we try to hide their presence in any country. Every seeker pair will only go to countries we are legally allowed into and will follow all local laws and customs while there. Each seeker pair will be required to speak the language and have a basic understanding of the local laws and culture before entering the country.

Once they return to the U.S. every seeker will spend the next six months combining and compiling all their data and looking for common traits and trends under the guidance of the Cabinet. At the end of six months, the findings will be brought to Congress and to me, your curious Dictator, for a full review.

Our country will use this data to help form new policies for the betterment of our nation. It will help guide us in our choices using data already generated from other countries experience. We *will* learn from the mistakes of others so we do not make them ourselves.

Like the census, we will do this every ten years.

IMMIGRATION

Before we start this discussion, let's begin with unless you are 100% Native American, **you** are an immigrant or the descendant of one. We all come from somewhere, but for most of us, it wasn't here. If we are to be truthful, your ancestors who first came to this country probably encountered the same kind of xenophobia people are heaping on the current round of immigrants. Every new wave of immigration throughout our history, no matter where they were from, were generally despised by the previous wave, now established in our society, the Irish, German, Polish, Asian, ad nausum. So, let's keep that in mind as we talk about immigration.

Now, I want to address a few other things when talking about people coming to our country. The first is, immigration to the U.S. is down and has been dropping for the last couple of years. Whatever you have been hearing from the fear-mongers, the numbers don't lie, immigration numbers are down across the board, and has been trending this way for the last several years. And the number of immigrants who have been here for over ten years are higher than those who have been here less than that. Which means, fewer new immigrants are coming in.

Second, unauthorized immigrants make up less than 4% of the population. Looking at that number alone should tell you if you lost your job, it's probably not because an immigrant took it, considering Americans and legal residents make up 96% of the population. Unless each and every one of them are trying to take ten or more jobs at a time, their employment will have very little impact on your ability to get a job.

Third, Mexicans do not make up the majority of unauthorized immigrants coming into our country. The majority are not crossing the Rio Grande to get here, they are coming in on planes and staying past their visas. A few take more unconventional routes, like in cargo containers, but again, those numbers are smaller than the ones who are waved through with visas in hand at airports.

Fourth, when it comes to crime, immigrants, whatever their status, are less likely to commit a crime than their native born neighbors. Homegrown crime is much more of a threat to you statistically than from someone foreign born. You can try and manipulate the data any way you'd like, but it's a fact, whether you like it or not. For that matter, you are more likely to be shot by a toddler in our country than a foreign terrorist. So, if you really need something to be afraid of, you should be more leery of a 2-foot toddler than a full grown terrorist, statistically speaking, of course.

Fifth, undocumented immigrants pay taxes, however they got here, and they are not using our social services, even though they are paying taxes. They add to our overall economic stability and to our GDP consumption, which in turn helps to increase profit margins for companies. They are not a drain on our society, they contribute to its well-being.

Now to address immigration. The process to legally get into our country is long, lengthy, convoluted, time-consuming and often disappointing, which is why some people choose to simply enter the country any way they can and take their chances. It can take up to 10 years to process a request to legally move to our country. That's a long time to wait if your life is in danger or circumstances have forced you to flee your country. Everybody wants a home, and nobody sane would choose to live in a refugee camp. If you were in similar circumstances, I imagine you would do the same.

Other factors are going to be putting more stress on not only our system, but many other countries in the near future, and the major one is global climate change. As sea levels rise and weather turns unpredictable, previously habitable regions, even within our own borders, will become uninhabitable, and we will need to address unfolding crisis going forward.

And lastly, we are going to have to take a long hard look in the mirror and acknowledge many of the refugees fleeing their countries is because of us. In places we have bombed back to the stone age, disrupted their economic structure, engaged in regime changes, imposed sanctions on, or let our corporations play havoc with their environment for profit, we have been a driving force behind much of the disruption around the world. We have to man up and acknowledge we played a hand in the current refugee crisis. We bear at least some of the responsibility for what has happened globally and we need to make it right somehow. Whether it is letting more refugees into our country or going to fix the mess we made so people can go home or something else entirely, we have to own what we have done and make amends.

IF I WERE DICTATOR

It's time for us to be the adults in the room, not the toddlers. Toddlers make messes and walk away unashamed, adults acknowledge the damage they have done and help fix the problem they created. It's time we grew up and accepted the responsibility for our actions.

Going forward, ICE will no longer spend their time looking for undocumented workers. If one commits an actual crime, ICE can step in and take appropriate measures, but if they aren't causing any trouble we're gonna let them be for the time being. We are instead going to shift our focus to immigration requests and improve the speed in which we process them.

Since many U.S. companies have a long history of hiring immigrants, both documented and undocumented, I want to bring those companies into the process. Someone looking to enter the country can begin the process using an authorized company as their way to legally enter the country. The company would be responsible for vetting each applicant and posting a bond for their good behavior while in the country. Each company would be responsible for each immigrant they vouch for and will submit all appropriate forms and information to Immigration prior to entry. The company would also be responsible for keeping track of each immigrant under their umbrella while in the country.

If, after two years, a company sponsored immigrant wishes to obtain permanent status in our country, they can begin the process. Provided they have had no legal troubles while in the country, have at least four members of the community vouch for their good character, and are in compliance with the work requirement.

If a company sponsored immigrant commits a serious crime while in the country, the company will be responsible for all legal compensation to the victim and lose the bond they posted. And, the person will be turned over to ICE agents to be dealt with.

For those who are already here, we need a plan that is compassionate and comprehensive. If you have been in the country for over 5 years, have not committed a crime of any kind, are a member in good standing with your community and a contributing member of society, you may apply for legal residence and cannot be deported unless you fail the background check.

Now, about the background checks. Not committing a crime is a good thing, but there is crime and then there is **crime**. If you were convicted of stealing to eat prior to entering our country, that doesn't hold the same weight as committing murder. Some crimes are only crimes in the country a person is from, and some have been forced into it because of circumstances because the option to opt out was not given. Child soldiers come to mind as I talk about this. There are places in this world, where young children are forced to become soldiers, often using family and fear to coerce compliance. Exceptions have to be made when warranted.

But if you have lived here and have become part of your community, we have to make allowances for how you came here to begin with. Entering illegally is frowned upon, but death on the other side of it, if forced to return, is neither right nor just. Give us your tired, your poor, your unwashed masses yearning to be free... we cannot turn our backs on those who have felt those words and came to our shores.

CHAPTER TWELVE
ELECTIONS

Elections. A dreaded and proud event in our country that has become a giant cluster in need of major sorting out. I may be your dedicated Dictator, but that doesn't mean I don't want you to have representation in your country and have your voice heard. As a matter of fact, I demand it.

In the 2016 election, 43% of eligible Americans didn't vote and another 38% of Americans are barred from voting altogether. That, my friend, is a horrifically high number. What those numbers tell me is it is not the average, middle of the road person choosing our representatives, but the ones who mostly pull hard left or right, the dedicated and the extremists. And you could see it reflected in the government we just dumped to the curb.

We don't want that to happen, ever again, it was a mess and no one listened to us and we were unhappy. So unhappy that in a poll, average Americans approved of body lice more than Congress. And let's face it, NOBODY *likes* body lice. In a true democracy, it shouldn't have been possible. If the government represented us, it would be around 25% off on the left, 25% off on the right, and the rest squarely in the moderate middle asking both sides to sit down and chill so we can get some things done.

So, in the spirit of true representation, I am now going to radically alter our election system, for you. Because I like you and want you to be happy.

Drum roll please...

Voting in elections is now mandatory and open to every American (waivers can be given for advanced age, infirmary or debilitating illness). When you sign up for UBI with the IRS you are also enrolled to vote and assigned a personal pin that will not change and will be used for every election. Since all of your data for living location is stored with the IRS, they will also designate your voting zone and send out notifications of when to vote in your area.

When setting up your voting data, you will then choose a

political affiliation: liberal, conservative, moderate, humanitarian, green, and labor. Affiliation can be changed once a year at your discretion.

When voting, you can choose to vote at a polling location or electronically with a confirmation of your vote and a copy of your selections sent to your email. If there are any discrepancies with your vote, you can flag your vote to have it investigated and corrected without delay.

But every American is entitled to participate in their government. Every law, every bill, every measure that is passed will have some effect on your life and you should have a say in how it will be governed.

There will also be new ethics requirements for anyone serving in any capacity in our government. For those of you familiar with the rules of conduct for student athletes, you will instantly recognize this. (Because seriously, how can you hold a college athlete to a higher standard of ethics than our state and federal officials???)

No official can accept gifts, money, lodging, food or freebies of any kind during their entire tenure in office. If they accept so much as a ham sandwich from anyone, they are immediately bounced out of office and replaced.

Congress will no longer be able to choose their own housing. Instead, apartments will be provided for each member of Congress similar to dome rooms in college. Apartments will be assigned by the housing monitor. If a representative wishes to bring their family with them, they will be given room to accommodate their family, or they can choose to not to, since they will spend half of their time back with their constituents in their home state. The government will pay for the representative's travel, but if they choose to bring their family, their transportation will be the responsibility of the individual representative.

Each of the rooms will come with its own private bath and adequate living space, but no kitchens. Meals will be provided on each floor in a communal kitchen. This is to encourage social interaction between representatives. It's harder to be hateful to someone you have to share a meal with daily.

Next item on the menu is pay. Congress, the Supreme Court, and the president's pay is now pegged to the average median wage. Nor is Congress allowed to raise their pay scale through legislation. The only way their pay can be increased is if the general public sees a corresponding wage increase.

Our government officials are there to serve us, the public. Not line their pockets with shows of favoritism or favors granted to selected individuals or industries.

Now, on to the rest of the changes by group.

THE PRESIDENT

Have you noticed when electing a president even if they get eight years, they spend two of those years running for re-election rather than running the country? Yeah, me too.

So, starting after I step down as your beloved Dictator, all presidential terms are for six years, and only six years. You have six whole years to guide the country and then you step down, like I did, gracefully and with dignity, as befits your office.

But we're not stopping there folks! There's more!

We're done with the parties controlling who will run and corporate interests determining how much money a candidate receives to do so. Instead, here is what we are going to do:

Round One:

Presidential elections begin at the state level a year before the final vote and each state will pick its own candidate.

To become eligible, you have to obtain the signatures of a minimum of 1% of the population of the state you are in, within three months of the start of the process. While campaigning to become your state's nominee, once you reach 1% of the population in signatures, you are now eligible to receive help from the government for your campaign. You will be given a set amount of free advertising for your message, and an assigned non-partisan staff who works for the election process, not the candidate. They will provide you with a set amount of funds and the manpower to send out fliers, posters, and other forms of contact to help people become aware of you and your message. They will also coordinate speaking events and debates with the other campaigns. Every eligible candidate will receive the same amount of staff, funding, and access.

Using a combination of tv advertising, yard signs, direct mailings, town hall meetings, and public debates, each potential president will have an equal chance to get their message out to the public. One caveat that should be noted, negative ads, of any kind, will not be allowed in our political system. A candidate must stand *for* something, not just against something. Nor can an outside third party promote any advertising for an individual candidate. Outside of inviting a candidate to speak at a public forum, there will be no other private citizen endorsement of any candidate using advertising.

You have three months to convince the people of your state, you're who they want before the state election. If there is only one who reaches 1% of the population, tag, they're it! If there is more than one, there will be a straight vote, whoever gets the most votes wins and goes on to the next round.

Round Two:
We now have 50 candidates to choose from. If it works for Miss America, it can work for president. Each candidate will be sorted according to political philosophy: liberal, conservative, moderate, humanitarian, green, and labor party. (Ah, now we see why I added that earlier)

Each candidate has three months to regale the public within their political party with their virtues as the next leader of the free world. Using their state staff, they can put up tv ads, engage in debates and rallies. At the end of three months, each election group will hold their own elections, and we are now down to six candidates for president.

Round Three:
For the next three months, up until a week before the election, each candidate will try to convince the majority of Americans they are the person for the job. There are no party votes, anyone can vote for whichever candidate they like the best. The one with the most votes wins. Duh. The runner up gets the vice-presidency.

But wait, there's more. You know those other four who didn't make it? They have a role to play as well. If they were popular enough to beat out 45 other people, then they obviously should have a place in our government. They will make up the beginnings of the new president's cabinet. Kept in the loop and consulted on policy.

But, they will have another role as well. Once a year after the election the American public will be given an opportunity to vote on how the president is doing with a simple up or down vote. If less than 45% of America gives the president a thumbs up, they are bumped out of office (good-bye have a nice life) and the vice-president becomes president and the third most popular candidate becomes vice-president. And this happens every year, giving the president motivation to give it their all, for all six years if they want to keep their job. Or, if for some reason the president feels he/she cannot stay in office, falls sick or dies, this gives the government a smooth transition of elected leaders as voted for by the entirety of the United States.

Okay, I think that about sums it up for president, let's move on to Congress, shall we?

THE HOUSE

The House is where we will now make a radical departure from how we choose our representatives. The House is supposed to be the people's house, the next step up from state and our middleman between federal and state. They are supposed to be our voices, representations of the general population, but that's not how it's worked out. We're going to change that now.

The House will hold no elections. Instead, every two years there will be a lottery, open to the public for anyone who is over 18, can pass a civics test, and is not currently incarcerated or on parole/probation can enter to become a part of Congress. If you wish to be a part of this process, you will need to submit your name, six months prior to upcoming selection, and must be done again with each new rotation if you wish to be in the lottery.

Because the House should represent the people they serve, half of the selected will be male, half female. In the case of transgenders, they will be considered whichever sex they identify with.

A House term will last four years, with half leaving every two years in rotation. This allows each representative the opportunity to earn measured authority going from junior to senior representative, yet provides enough restraint that no single person could force their counterparts into compliance without reasonable adherence to reasoned argument.

During the transition year, the senior members of the House will vote on who will be the new Speaker of the House.

After serving your four years, you have to wait at least four years before joining the lottery again.

Beginning with the first selection of House Representatives, all U.S. territories will have voting representation. The days of non-voting representatives are a thing of the past. Anyone living in a U.S. territory is a U.S. citizen and will be given the same rights, respect, and representation as any other citizen.

In case of an ethics violations in the House, an immediate new lottery selection will be held and a replacement placed in office within two weeks.

In case of an ethics violation in the Senate, the Speaker of the House will be moved over to fill the vacancy, a new Speaker of the House elected and a new lottery selection will be installed as a House representative within two weeks.

In case of ethics violations by the president, the previously discussed rules will apply to the vice-president moving up to fill the position.

Since this will be by lottery, the first selection of half the House electorate will begin on November 11th the first year after I am in office. Two years after that, the other half will be elected, after that the normal rotation will go into effect.

THE SENATE

There will be changes made to the Senate, but not as many as we made with the House. Senators will serve one eight year term, and like the House will stagger rotate out every four years. Senators may only serve once in their lifetime. As in the House, we will have equality in representation, one Senator will always be male, the other female. In the case of transgenders, the same rule as in the House applies.

Those wishing to serve will follow the same general principles we use to elect our president. An individual will need to procure signatures of 1% of the population of their state within three months of the official beginning of the election cycle date. If they reach the threshold, they are officially in the running and will be assigned a staff from the elections commission.

You now have three months to convince people you should be their Senator. Your staff will coordinate with the other hopefuls and provide an equal amount of airtime, advertising, rallies, and debates between the candidates to give each candidate a fair and equal chance of wooing the voters. There are no party line votes, vote for whoever you want, and the one with the most votes wins.

Because of the staggered nature of the process, I, as your compassionate Dictator, will choose the first 50 Senators, 25 males, and 25 females. Their tenure will begin within six months after I attain office. I will choose one person from each state who has been recognized as a humanitarian, civil rights advocate, community organizer, economist, historian or some other civic minded individual.

Beginning four years after I started office, we will hold our first Senate election and elect our next 50 representatives for office. If I chose a male for a state, then that state will be electing a female, and the flip if I chose a female.

Choose wisely, my friends.

U.S. SUPREME COURT

Okay, let's get serious here for a moment, nobody, and I mean nobody, needs to be placed in a lifetime appointment. I will concede, for the Supreme Court to be as neutral as possible, it should have a long tenure, but not a lifetime. So, with that in mind, I as your beloved Dictator, do so declare the Supreme Court tenure is reduced to 20 years. It is long enough to provide the country with stability and short enough our laws retain some flexibility in interpretation.

There will also be changes to how they are chosen, and we can begin this process as soon as we have a sitting Congress. For the initial round, each state Legal Board will choose a sitting judge they feel embodies the traits of a fair, flexible, legal mind who understands Constitutional law. Once the states have picked their nominee, they will be sent to the House. The House will then select three qualified judges from each political affiliation: liberal, conservative, moderate, humanitarian, green, and labor. Those selections will be sent on to me, your humble Dictator to chose one judge from each affiliation. And we now have our first new Supreme Court.

The first Supreme Court will not serve out their full 20 years because we want them to be staggered. They will all serve for the first 4 years, at the end of 4 years, the oldest serving judge will be retired and replaced with someone from their political affiliation. Two years after that the next oldest will be replaced and so on down the line, always with a judge from their political affiliation.

The process for Supreme Court selections after the initial picks will be, the states will select one qualified judge to nominate, but one only from the affiliation that is being replaced. Those 50 nominees will again be sent to House and they will pick 25 judges they deem qualified for the job. Those 25 will be sent on to the Senate to be vetted and they will choose 5 nominees to send on to the president. The president will pick the next judge from those 5 nominees. That judge will immediately become the next Supreme Court judge with no other input from Congress.

No more stalling out nominees in hearings. No more patrician politics. Each judge will go through an ever narrower selection process with the state judicial boards, the House, and the Senate all having input along the way by the time it reaches the president's desk. Having a judge from each political affiliation ensures every group in America is represented and the rotation ensures the court does not stagnate with age.

We will also be going through all the pending legal arguments that were interrupted by our revolution. They will temporarily be put on hold as we start our transition period and exam many of the laws we have on the books to see if they are something we even want to keep. I will be instituting a process to purge unnecessary and/or cruel and inhuman laws and we'll get into that later on in *Legal Stuff*.

JUDGESHIPS

For more years than is right or healthy for a functioning democracy of laws, many state and district court judges have been left unfilled, causing a backlog of cases and our legal system to lag behind. These lags should not be tolerated, affecting the lives of Americans as they await their day in court. The Sixth Amendment requires the courts provide a quick and speedy trial, but defendants sometimes wait years for their cases to be heard in court due to backlog. This is unacceptable.

Since the idea of people sitting and waiting years to be seen before a judge offends my basic sensibilities, we are going to address this, and quickly. As mentioned before, there will be a purging of laws, and some defendants may simply be released if they are awaiting trial due to the changing laws. But for the rest, I promise we will get to you as soon as humanly possible.

To help fill these positions, it is no longer going to be the sole responsibility of the president to appoint court of appeals judges or district court judges. Each state or district using their Legal Board will select 10 judges they deem qualified for the position. Those 10 selections will be passed on to the House, where they will select 5 judges who will then be vetted by the Senate and will pick 2 nominees to send on to the president who will choose one. They will begin their position within 15 days of confirmation by the president.

Until the Senate is up and running, and to ensure our courts are fully staffed, I as your dedicated Dictator, do so decree the following. The state or district Legal Board will appoint qualified judges to fill all empty seats to get our legal system up and running. Anyone appointed to the bench will not serve more than 3 years without going through the full confirmation procedure, if that judge is approved, they may serve out their remaining time. Once the Senate is up and running, as each seat becomes open, the new process will be instituted.

No judge below Supreme Court can hold a particular appointed office for more than ten years at a time.

Judges' salaries shall be pegged at the median average wage of their state or district.

LOCAL & STATE ELECTIONS

Local and state elections will remain largely unaffected. But that doesn't mean we can't make a few improvements to them. One of those areas of improvement is how we currently draw our district lines. This has been an ongoing issue for many years when we had a two party system and each side tried to draw districts that favored them when given the chance. We need to stop giving any side an advantage over another when it comes to our elections. They should fairly reflect the people they are representing.

So, with this thought in mind, I hereby decree as your concerned Dictator, state districts will now be drawn according to counties. Counties cannot be broken up, and each State Representative will represent either a single county or a block of counties in neighboring groups for more sparsely populated areas. We'll work to make this as fair as possible, and ensures each group receives an equal voice in how their state is run.

But from here, I would like to turn to community leaders, community organizers, and others who have been working for many years to ensure all our voices can be heard, and help bring this dream to reality. I'm counting on you to work with me and together to make our country a true democracy where each of us matters and each vote counts. If you have a better idea than the dividing districts by counties, I will be more than happy to hear your suggestions and put them to good use.

And that's where I'm going to leave these local elections, in your hands. So, think it over, talk with your colleagues, and bring me a plan that is fair for all.

THE ELECTION COMMITTEE

The election committee is going to be one of the most important agencies in our country. This is the board that will ensure fair and equal treatment to each candidate and keep our democracy safe from meddling.

The election committee will be responsible for each voting district they work in, ensuring the voting process goes smoothly and without outside pressure or influence. To reflect the importance of this, the National Director of the election committee will be given a position in the presidential Cabinet. For our government to work as it should, the people must be heard.

The election committee will be primarily made up of full time government employees. Candidates may come and go, but the election committee will go on unaffected by wins or losses. Each committee will be made up of a variety of employees who will be responsible for advertising, coordinating and planning events, budgeting, and all the other details that go with a public campaign from local to federal levels.

All elections will be financed by the government, through our taxes. Private donations to any candidate will no longer be legal and will be considered a bribe and prosecuted as such. Part of the duties of the committee will be to watch over the financial transactions of candidates and if any candidate is found to have received illicit money, to remove them from running immediately.

The committee is also charged with investigating any reports of sitting representatives accepting money or bribes of any kind during their tenure. If an investigation finds either money or other gifts were exchanged, they are to turn over all evidence to their state's attorney for prosecution for treason against the State. Our representatives work for the people, all of the people, and if they take a bribe or engage in illicit activity, they are working against the best interests of the people, and should be held accountable for their actions. Ethics and legal violations in the House and Senate will no longer be under the purview of Congress to investigate. It will be a legal matter for the state the representative came from to determine, and representatives will be judged by a jury of their peers, from a pool of people in their district.

In a case of illicit activities by the president, vice-president, or president in waiting, cases will be heard in Federal court by the U.S. District Court in D.C.

To be a functional democracy we need to have faith in our election process and our representatives. Making our elections safe, fair, and unblemished by bribery or favoritism will go a long way towards restoring the people's faith in their government.

CHAPTER THIRTEEN
LEGAL STUFF

As much as I personally love chaos there does need to be some order, some structure, for our society to hang its collective hat on to function. But, I also believe we have too many laws right now to function effectively and many of them seem designed for the sole purpose of putting people in jail so that a very few can profit from the pain of incarceration. We need a bit more common sense when it comes to our laws and it is my hope, and with your help, we can correct the many wrongs committed in our country's judicial system.

Our laws should be there to protect us, not make us afraid or make our lives harder than they already are. Our police force should be part of our community, and looked at as friends, not adversaries, as they often are now, and it is our laws that have made it this way. In many cases, it's not bad officers, but bad laws they uphold that causes the conflict.

Our legal system has drifted away from the core of what it should represent, the protective line between our citizens and harm. It's nothing more complicated than that, but we have added layer after layer of rules and laws that do not uphold this idea. Instead, we have a putative aspect that is more concerned with vengeance, generating money or protecting corporate interests over protecting individuals from harm. We must end this practice. Our country has more people incarcerated per capita, than any other nation on earth. We have more people in our legal system than China, Iran, or any other despot dictatorship in the world. How can we call ourselves the land of the free when 1 out of every 110 are in jail, and 1 out of every 51 are on parole or probation?

We have over 2.2 million people incarcerated at any given time in our country, and those numbers are rising, not falling. And yet, violent crime has been falling steadily for the last quarter century, a decrease of 50% between 1993 and 2015. The greatest increase in incarceration has been in non-violent crime, going from 16% in 1970 to our current situation of over 50% for mostly low-level drug offenses. We are devastating entire communities and ruining lives on a daily basis with our excessive, and often over the top, punitive laws. It has to stop.

We are spending so much money on punishing people we have taken away money from the things that actually address crime prevention, such as education, poverty, and desperation. You sometimes hear someone ask, "Would you steal to save the life of a loved one?" We all know the answer, of course, we would all answer "Yes." Because we value the life of a loved one, over a law that keeps us from saving them. And when it comes to low-level non-violent crime, you will find it is more often desperation at the core of their actions, not animosity.

As many of my proposals are put into place, such as UBI, increases in education access, universal healthcare, and other programs designed to improve our overall life situation, crime will begin to naturally fall even lower. Outside of some white-collar crime based on greed, most people who have the basics of a good life generally don't become desperate enough to commit crimes. There's not enough gain to make it worth the risk. The best way to bring about a safe and stable society is to address those ills, not punitively punish those who have fallen victim to an injustice system.

Before becoming your beloved Dictator, I spent the last decade helping people by taking in the homeless, the helpless, the desperate and downtrodden, and given them a place within my home to get back on their feet and rebuild their lives. I have seen firsthand how our system has failed us, over and over again, and stared into the cracks that allowed so many to fall through into desperation and hopelessness. I have taken in vets, pregnant women, ex-cons, recovering addicts and sometimes entire families, and 95% of the time, they have gone on to better lives because I gave them a second chance after they lost everything. So, I know personally how much a helping hand can make a difference.

On my own, and out of my own pocket, I have helped hundreds who would otherwise been lost. And now, with your help, I would like to save millions. I would like to give all of us a second chance at a better life, a life we can each be proud of, pursuing happiness without fear of falling through the cracks of a fractured society. I want every American citizen to live a life that is safe, secure, and stable, to become the best versions of ourselves and be the shining example of hope for the rest of the world we've always claimed to be, but never quite achieved.

I want us to truly be the land of the free and to do that, we must change our laws. We must go back to the idea of protection from harm, not punitive punishment for mishap. I will need all of you to help, and bring to our collective attention those things needing addressed, and work together to change our country for the better, for all of us. So, let us begin with *Simplifying the Legal Code.*

SIMPLIFYING THE LEGAL CODE

Because our country is full of laws, some punitive without purpose, some contradictory, and some just plain silly, the best place to begin is simplifying our laws. I would like to set up an advisory board in every state with a mix of attorneys, civil right activists, historians, and sociologist to go over every law in their state and review them. At the top of this list, we should begin with "blue" laws, you know the ones I'm talking about, the ones that make absolutely no sense, yet there they are anyway. Like, you can't fish from horseback in Washington D.C. or a man can't knit during fishing season in New Jersey. They're funny, don't get me wrong, but they have no business being in our legal code.

I believe our laws should follow a very simple code, if it's not stealing, it should be legal. Kidnapping = stealing a person. Murder = stealing a life. You get the idea. I realize large groups of people living together needs to have some flexibility when it comes to enacting laws, but too many of our laws are there for the sole purpose of giving a relatively small group of people vast amounts of power, legally. Citizen United comes to mind, a law allowing unlimited amounts of money to flow through our system with no oversight, stealing the voices away from the many so only a few (very rich) are heard.

Perhaps the most important point we need to address is our two-tiered legal system. One code of accountability for the rich, and another for the rest of us. This needs to end. And we need to address the slap-on-the-wrist policy towards white-collar crime vs. decades in prison for a crime that harmed no one if you're poor. We are one country, under one set of laws, that no one should be above. The legal loopholes that have allowed corporations, banks, and Wall Street to break the law with impunity will be closed.

There is no difference between stealing someone's money at gunpoint or through deception of computer code, and our laws should reflect that. Throughout the years our country has suffered because of this two-tiered system allowing those with money to run roughshod over those of us who don't. They have collapsed our entire economy and walked away unscathed for their deceptions

IF I WERE DICTATOR 185

beyond a stern, "Don't do it again." and a small monetary fine for their behavior.

We will have sanity in our legal system and bring it back to where it should be, the fine line between us and harm. No more, and no less.

NOSY NEIGHBOR LAWS

Our country is currently loaded down with what I consider *Nosy Neighbor* laws. These are laws attempting to control a person's private life so they behave in a way that is more comfortable for someone else. These are laws, designed not to prevent harm or bolster the public good, but simply control behavior, often based on religious beliefs rather than secular need.

These are laws about how many vibrators an individual can own. Or if who they love is legal. Or if the body they inhabit is their own or belongs to the state. These are laws only because someone was uncomfortable with a lifestyle or people making personal choices they may not like, not because it was bringing any harm to the general public. So, let me be very clear on this, from this day forward every person in our country has body autonomy. Nor can any law be made to restrict body autonomy, unless it can be shown it will cause actionable harm to others.

For those of you who skipped over this in other sections, I'm going to reiterate what body autonomy is because it is important. Each person has the right to decide what goes in, on, around, over, carried by, or through their body, without interference from another human being. Your body belongs to you. Not to the state. Not to your spouse. It is the only thing on this earth that truly belongs to you, and you are the only one who has to deal with it from birth to death, so it is yours to decide what to do with it.

Now, I will concede an exception to this rule. For minors, there will be some oversight by their parent or guardian as to what can and cannot be done. As an example, vaccinations are important, and just because a child doesn't like them (who likes shots?) because it is in their best interest, and for society at large, to be vaccinated, a child cannot invoke body autonomy to get out of being inoculated. Because minors, especially young minors, are not always capable of making rational nor reasoned choices, a parent or guardian has the right to step in and save them from the folly of their potentially bad choices.

So, with this in mind, I, as your loving Leader, do hereby decree all personal behavior laws are stricken from the books, with a few caveats. If your personal behavior endangers another human being, you will be held accountable for your lapse in judgment. You may drink yourself stupid, but if you neglect your children or get behind the wheel of a vehicle, etc. you will be held accountable. You may use any drug you want, but again, if you endanger another human being's life or welfare, you will be held accountable. But as long as you are doing no harm, then you are free to be you.

In relation to this, the legal age for any mind altering drug, including alcohol, will be dropped down to 18. If you are considered adult enough to join the military, carry a weapon, and even die for your country, then you are old enough to decide if you want to drink or not. Under 18, a child over the age of 14 may have a limited amount of alcohol or marijuana under the supervision of a parent or guardian. Other countries have allowed this and it has not ended in a country full of addicts, our society will survive.

Want to own 400 vibrators? Go for it. Want to watch porn? Feel free to be sticky. Want to knit during fishing season? Who am I to say how to best spend your free time? Want to tattoo your entire body? Enjoy the artwork, but might I suggest you pick a good tattoo artist, I'd hate for you to be stuck with crappy art for the rest of your life. Marry the person of your choice or even marry the people of your choice, enjoy your life and love who you want, it's none of my business, nor of your neighbors or the governments. Your body is your temple, and it can be a shining monolith or a crumbling husk of a shell, whatever you choose to do with it.

From here on out, a law can only be made if it shows the public good it brings overshadows the curbing of individual rights. But what we read, watch, imbibe, consume, or engage in cannot be infringed upon unless actionable harm can be shown. A how-to guide on building a nuclear bomb probably shouldn't be up for public consumption, but talking about it, without giving schematics or specifics on how to make one, is perfectly okay. And I realize, even a spoon can be deadly in the wrong hands, so we're going to have to use common sense here, as painful as that might be for some of us.

And I realize some things are questionably murky, such as the many drugs that are available from alcohol to heroin, or previous laws prohibiting prostitution, but whenever we create laws to curb these activities with punitive penalties, we have always failed. We are better off putting laws in place to keep the general public safe, offer support services for those who want it, regulate it in a sane manner, and tax it when we can.

In our history, many of the laws we have enacted were not for general safety, which should be the primary purpose of any law. Instead, our country has tried to legislate our souls, usually out of good intentions, but that's still not a good enough reason to do it. So I want all of us to start saying, "If it doesn't affect me personally, it's none of my business." or, if this works better for you, "Not my circus. Not my monkeys." What your neighbors, friends, family, or other random strangers do behind closed doors or to their own body, is none of your concern. Let each of us be able to pursue happiness without prosecution. The sooner we stop being nosy neighbors trying to make others abide by our personal sense of "goodness" the faster we can actually be the nation of freedom we claim to be.

PATENT LAWS

You may be wondering why I've given patent laws its own space while lumping other laws all together. It comes down to this, our patent laws, as they are now, are stifling innovation in our country. It is not uncommon for a company to buy the patent for something that would create competition in their area, and then just sit on the idea, forever. There are thousands of patents accumulating dust that will never see the light of day, simply because a corporation put their profits before people, again.

This practice will end. From here on out, if a company purchases a patent from an individual or group, they will be required to implement the patent within 5 years. If they do nothing with it, the patent will revert back to public domain and anyone can use the idea and profit from it. Nor will the company be able to recoup the price they paid for it from the originator if they lose the patent. I want innovation encouraged in this country, not stifled by corporate interests.

One other quick mention about patents and corporations. If an idea is patented that does not violate a company's patents, but has the potential to interfere with its profits, they're going to have to suck it up. With the changes to our laws, we're going to make it impossible to sue someone for "interference with potential profits" or anything remotely resembling those words. We need healthy competition in this country, and it will be encouraged, not sued out of existence by established corporations fearful of losing profits because of a better, cheaper, easier idea.

As with most things in this book, I am open to suggestions and how to best go about enforcing this, and even modifications made to the basic idea. But, I will stand firm on the bedrock of the idea, patents will be used or they will be public domain, no one will be allowed to slow our progress because of greed.

Now, if a patent is found to be dangerous to the public, and a corporation brings to the Department of Commerce a particular idea or innovation which may have damaging ramifications to the public good, the Commerce Department will purchase the patent for the price the company paid for it and not allow it back into the public domain. If after investigation, Commerce concurs with their assessment.

Sometimes, as humans, we think more about what we can do, rather than what we should do. And innovation can be wonderful, but it can also be deadly, and we need to make sure we are not adding to the general misery when we create something. It's a faded, tattered line to be walked, too much oversight inhibits our creative abilities, not enough, and we could get something that ends all life on this planet as we know it. And neither of those two extremes are good for us as a society, so we're going to have to accept that all we can do is our best, while making the laws as flexible as possible and using common sense whenever we can.

LAW ENFORCEMENT & US

Let me preface this section with, I know most law enforcement officers are good people. My father was a cop and I grew up around other officers and I know this to be true. That being said, the few bad apples, combined with arbitrary laws and the militarization of our police force, have begun to pit our police against the general public welfare. To *protect and serve* is the motto of the police force, not *intimidate and incarcerate*. The police are there to serve the public good, but when we stray from that we get the mess we're currently in.

In 2017, 964 people were killed by police officers. Sadly, there are no numbers, or reporting systems to give you the number of non-fatal shootings by the police. That, in and of itself, is pretty scary. Nor is there any comprehensive official reporting of fatal shootings, those numbers I gave you are basically just people going through the papers and counting the numbers of deaths reported in connection with a police department. The CDC is not even allowed to track gun deaths, or collect any information about guns in general, so there are no reliable numbers we can point to. This is simply not acceptable.

To change this around we're going to begin with training. We need better training for our officers, and we need to make training and education an on-going part of the job. Learning proper de-escalation procedures in times of crisis is going to be a must. Reaching for a weapon should always be the last resort after all other options have been extinguished. I understand being a police officer can be a dangerous job, then again, it doesn't even make the top 10 list of the most dangerous jobs in the U.S. It's more dangerous to be a landscaper than it is to be an officer of the law. That's not to say every day when an officer puts on their uniform they aren't putting their lives at risk, but so is every fisherman who goes out on a boat.

How our officers are educated will be changing and no longer focused primarily on tactical training, but will include basic psychology, crowd management, crisis assessment, ethics of policing, abuse response and victim assessment, basic law and judicial practices, just to name a few. Before anyone can put on a uniform, a degree in law enforcement will be required as we go forward. Learning on the job, or figuring it out as we go, or winging it won't cut it anymore. Every officer will be highly trained, educated, and ready for the responsibility the uniform comes with to deal effectively with the public without threat or excessive force.

There will need to be a weeding out of those few bad apples in our police force. The specific process for that, I am going to leave to others with more expertise in these matters. But the requirements for becoming an officer will be applied universally and in every department in this country, whatever its size, will be mandatory. The job of an officer is a weighty responsibility, and as a country, we should demand every officer is qualified to hold the position.

Yearly psych evaluations will also be made mandatory to ensure every officer on the streets is not suffering from anything that would prevent them from acting in the best interest of the public while on the job. There will also be a comprehensive reporting system for every time an officer unholsters a gun, fires a round, or shoots someone, whether it is fatal or not. Every department will be required to submit monthly reports on arrests as well, and include such information as the type of crime and what gender, age and race the arrestee was. If a department seems to be trending toward any type of profiling, action will be taken to address and correct the situation.

All military grade weapons will be returned to the federal government and no longer allowed in civilian hands, even if those hands carry a badge. One of my favorite quotes about military and law enforcement is from Admiral Adama, "*There's a reason you separate military and the police. One fights the enemies of the state, the other serves and protects the people. When the military becomes both, then the enemies of the state tend to become the people.*" This goes for turning our police officers into paramilitary units as well, I do not want our police to see the people they are supposed to protect as the enemy they must combat.

All racial profiling will end. If a black man is walking down the street of a mostly white neighborhood you are patrolling, you smile and wave as you pass, unless you have a damned good reason to stop them. Like they're waving a gun in the air or holding a screaming hostage. A person is innocent until proven guilty, period.

Civil forfeitures are a thing of the past. If you can't come up with enough evidence to charge a person in a court of law and get a guilty verdict, they, and all of their possessions, are innocent. Nor will money or goods taken in convicted criminal cases be left with the stations that brought it in. Those items will be sent on to the state where they will be auctioned off quarterly and added to the general fund to be distributed evenly. But nothing can be touched until a guilty verdict has been pronounced.

Monthly or yearly quotas are also going to be a thing of the past. Police stations will no longer get incentives for the number of arrests they make or tickets they give out. Instead, the station with the lowest crime numbers per capita each month will receive a small bonus as a reward. If you want to be rewarded, keep the peace, not create crime.

Another practice that we will be curtailing is bail. Over 70% of people sitting in jail haven't been convicted of a crime, they simply couldn't come up with the money to get out. So they have to wait in jail for their day in court, which can sometimes take years. Studies have shown bail is not a deciding factor in whether or not someone shows up for court. A reminder by a court officer by phone 24 hours before a court date, on the other hand, is effective. No one should have to sit in jail only because they were broke, nor should a family have to remortgage their home to bail a loved one out of jail. And if someone is thought to be too dangerous to be let out while awaiting trial, then they shouldn't be able to get out no matter how much money they have.

The practice of putting someone in jail for failure to pay a fine will also come to an end. Excessive punitive fines have not shown to be effective in cutting down on civil law violations. And sending someone to jail for being poor helps no one. Community service will become the new standard for minor and mid-level civil law violations rather than monetary fines. Nor will our courts be allowed to criminally prosecute low-level debt on behalf of a collection agency with jail time or excessive fines.

I want our citizens to see police officers as a force for good in our communities, not the enemy. There will be other changes as time goes on to make our police force more responsive to public need, but this is where we will start.

Our prison system is in need of a major overhaul, and we will begin with the abolition of the for-profit prison system. While capitalism has its place in our society, in our legal system, it does not. No one should profit off the misery of others, and the for-profit prison system is a prime example of predatory practices overwhelming public good. When laws are made to satisfy corporate quotas over public good, you know something is very, very wrong with our system.

With our laws being overhauled, we will also be reviewing prison rolls and begin releasing inmates if they were incarcerated using now defunct laws. Review boards will be set up and each prisoner's file will be reviewed using the new criteria for incarceration, if they do not meet it, they will be released, and their record expunged of the charge(s).

Facilities will be set up to help with reintegration into society. Temporary housing will be given to those who do not have a support network to return to, and each person will be assigned a caseworker who will help them set up their UBI, find housing, get all their needed ID's and help them work out a life-plan to get back into the swing of being a free person. The primary goal is to help each individual thrive in our new society, to feel they are an active and welcome member of it so they do not fall into desperate habits. Counseling, both personal or drug related, will be available as well to help with the transition.

Assuming a 39% to 51% reduction in our prison population, we can quickly empty the for-profit prisons and those remaining prisoners can be moved to public prisons run by either the federal or state government, or the government can purchase those private prisons if it is deemed necessary, if a reasonable price can be negotiated.

Now, as your benevolent Dictator, I am now going to change the very concept of what prison is. We are no longer going to be warehousing prisoners for punitive punishment. In most cases, after serving their time, prisoners will be released back into society, where they will become our neighbors and co-workers. They are going to be a part of our society, so it is in our best interest not to make them hardened, but rehabilitate them while they are incarcerated.

I am going to draw heavily on Norway's prison model for reshaping our system. They have a proven model with the lowest reincarnation rates in the world and I want to bring it here to the US. The core of every prison will be rehabilitation, not punishment. The punishment is the loss of their freedom, it should not be their humanity. In fact, it is their humanity I wish to encourage, to nurture in each individual and help them become a productive and stable member of our society.

We will begin by rebuilding when necessary or remodeling when possible, our prisons to make them less like cages and more homelike. If we treat people like animals, why should we be surprised when they act like animals? So, we will create comfortable accommodations for each prisoner, complete with a private bathroom in each room, and a door instead of bars for entry. We will no longer be stacking people like cargo, creating cramped and uncomfortable conditions caused by overcrowding. I want the prisoners to have a place to relax, feel safe, and begin the process of habitation without fear.

Okay, I can see your eyerolls from this side of my words right now. "*Why should we treat them with respect if they had no respect for us?*" is probably running through your head right now. Because, one day most will walk among us again, and for us to be safe, we have to treat them as people, not animals, so when they get out, they can act like people. Again, this is about rehabilitation, not vengeance.

Our prisons will no longer be storage facilities where we lock people up and forget about them, but a place they can learn from their mistakes and find ways to correct them before they are released again. Prison sentences will no longer be made on an arbitrary measure of time, but when they are deemed able to safely be released by a panel of specialists. The point of all of this is to make them better so they no longer feel the need to hurt others. In certain cases, where habitation is not an option, they will be kept indefinitely, for their safety and ours. But when a prisoner is no longer deemed a threat to society, they will be released. If they prefer to stay a hardened criminal, then they can spend the rest of their life confined to a prison without means of release.

But never again will someone dangerous be let out because of an arbitrary measurement of time imposed by a judge. Nor will someone who is no danger to others be allowed to rot in jail because of that same arbitrary system. The new system will be there for everyone's protection.

Each prisoner will essentially be in control of their own release. If they are willing to fix the things wrong inside them that caused them to act out, and are judged safe to return to society without threat, they can be released. If they refuse, they can rot in jail. It's entirely up to the individual. Prisoners will no longer just be marking the days until they are released since the timescale for their release is dependent on them getting better and no longer posing a threat to society. If it takes them 10 years, then that's how long it takes, and not a day less. But they will no longer be able to sit in jail and do nothing while counting down the days.

There will also be a monitoring program in place after their release, as both a guide and a check on their behavior for a year after release, as was described above when talking about reintegration. The goal is not to catch them in bad behavior to send them back into the prison system, but catch them before they do anything harmful and redirect them, if possible, to more constructive behavior.

To begin this healing process, each prisoner will begin therapy with a qualified therapist who can address their specific issues and help overcome them. Group therapy will also be used, and encouraged, as part of the process. Service animals may also be utilized if it is deemed appropriate. Healing old wounds that have warped a person's sense of self, and is a primary factor in violent crimes, will be paramount. No prisoner will be released until they have been cleared by the psychologist and the team in charge of each prisoner's care.

Education will be an important part of the process as well. Whether it is gaining a high school diploma, learning a trade, or earning a degree. Education can be an integral part of a person's self-worth, encouraging each prisoner to expand their knowledge and learn a trade or earn a degree will serve them well once they are released. If a prisoner has a degree, is a competent tradesman or has a teachable talent, they will be encouraged to share their knowledge while they are incarcerated by teaching classes and sharing what they know.

Hobbies will also be encouraged, art, music, writing, woodworking, and other forms of self-expression will be part of their rehabilitation. As will leisure pursuits such as reading, knitting, coloring, or listening to music will be a part of each of their days.

Yoga will become a mandatory part of the daily routine, and classes will be given three times a day, and depending on the person's temperament, they will choose which time to join. Yoga encourages relaxation, self-reflection, and self-awareness, something we want each prisoner to engage in.

Classes in life skills will be given if deemed necessary by their caseworkers. These will be classes on how to move through society and know how to behave in social situations many find awkward if it was not a part of their daily life before incarceration. Things like dressing appropriately for a job interview, how to fill out a job application, understanding credit and using credit cards competently, and learning to budget time and money. It will also be proper dinner etiquette, small talk, even dancing lessons. All the small things we should all know as functional adults, but sadly, many of us lack when we venture forth into the real world and suddenly find ourselves floundering for our lack.

Family is important, and cutting a prisoner off from family is a mistake. Having a strong support network is crucial in reducing reincarceration rates. To encourage this, each prison will have comfortable lounges for families to gather and interact without bars or glass between them. Comfortable and soothing accommodations that encourage people to relax, not cold plastic or antiseptic environments that put people on edge. Appropriate physical contact will be allowed as well, hug your kids, kiss your spouse, give grandma a peck on the cheek.

Family services will also be offered during a family member's incarceration. Counseling will be offered, both individually, and family sessions with their incarcerated member involved. Working out family issues and conflicts is an important part of the healing process, not just for the prisoner, but for their family as well. A family member going to prison can be devastating to everyone and addressing this is an important factor in the healing process. Other family needs will also be addressed by an assigned caseworker whose goal is to help keep the family together and functioning during this time.

My goal, as your dedicated Dictator, is to do everything we can to bring down the rates of incarceration in our nation without increasing the crime rates. Rehabilitation, education and, reintegration is the key to that. To address all the ills of our prison system will take reams of paper, far beyond this general guideline I am presenting you with right now. It will take all of us to fix what is wrong and make it right, and I hope I have your support in this.

No one should lose their freedom because they could not pay a fine. And no prisoner should ever be made to feel less than human if we ever want to end this cycle of incarceration our nation has been on for over a decade now. We need to look at each other with compassion and understanding, tempered with common sense. Not everyone who commits a crime is inherently "bad", in most cases crime comes from desperation, and once we begin to correct the underlying causes of it, we can all live in a better, safer, world.

MOBS & GANGS

Organized crime and gang activity have been a part of our culture for a while now. It can seem like it is a problem that will never go away, and only getting worse for those who live with the threat of some organized criminal activity nearby.

I don't have any super solutions to this problem, but I do have some common sense thoughts about it, and it seemed appropriate to address them here in *Legal Stuff*.

Most criminal activities have been supported by illicit activity such as drugs and prostitution. Since I made both of those things legal, and now under state and federal regulation for oversight and taxation, they won't be all that lucrative for much longer as a criminal activity.

When it comes to gang activity, poverty has been their greatest recruitment tool, alongside desperation and lack of options for employment or education. Since I have addressed these ills and we are working on changing those situations, gaining new recruits will be a harder sell as well. The year of giving will also help break this chain of recruitment. As young adults are sent out of their neighborhoods to help others while learning new skills and making new friends, will all help alleviate the entrenched hopelessness that poverty, isolation, and desperation can bring, and gangs used to their advantage.

Cleaning up neighborhoods, providing education, employment, a basic standard of living allowance, upgrading failing systems, better school education, and access to medical care will all go toward making life better for everyone, including those who have turned to crime when a better life seemed denied to them because of circumstance and birthplace. Giving people a feeling of worth, of community, and of value will go a long way towards ending gang and mob violence because the factors that made them their only viable option are now gone. And the activities that once supported their organizations are part of the public venue.

I don't believe we will ever be able to bring the crime rates down to zero, as much as I would like to think it is possible, human nature being what it is, does have its bad apples. But doing all the things we have discussed in this book will bring crime down overall and make our society safer for it. Individually, we may feel powerless, but together we can correct what needs to be fixed and make our country a better place when we are done.

A FINAL FAREWELL

Alas, dear friends, we have reached the end of our journey together. It has been scary, infuriating, uplifting, exciting, and productive, and now we are about to part ways. I want to say thank you, to each and every one of you, who made this journey with me. And I hope, even after you close this book you will continue what we started together, working to make the world, and our country, a place we are proud to call home.

This is, of course, not a full list of everything that needs our attention in our country, but a bare bones outline of some of our most pressing problems. It does not address the Patriot Act, nor any of the subsequent legislation that was born from it. Guantanamo and its terrible legacy or "enhanced" integration that has faded in and out of popularity in our leadership (I'm completely against it, if you were wondering).

Nor did we talk about increasing funding for NASA or research for space exploration. Another problem for another day is the ring of junk currently circling our planet and threatening satellites, the space station, and occasionally the planet below, and what to do about it.

And we only briefly touched on such topics as systemic racism, homophobia, woman's rights, domestic violence, and our country's chronic xenophobia. All of which we need to talk about and work on practical solutions that allow all Americans to live together in relative peace and full equality. No matter how uncomfortable the conversation makes us.

This book addresses just a few of the problems our country will have to face if we are ever to go forward into a brighter future. But we can't become so overwhelmed by the problems that we can't look for solutions, one step at a time. Know each step forward is one more thing we can cross off our list before we tackle the next problem.

As I said in the beginning, I do not have all the answers. It will be up to all of us to find those answers together. Sometimes we may stumble, or choose unwisely, but as long as we continue going forward, we can change the world for the better. As individuals, it can seem like an impossible task, but you found me, and while you may not have agreed with everything in this book, you found enough common ground with me to continue reading until the end, or you wouldn't be here, and now we are no longer alone, we have each other. But it doesn't have to stop here with just the two of us, because there are more like us out there, we just need to find them.

Some may say this book is about entitlement, thinking the world owes us something for nothing. But I say, the better way to look at this is, what do we owe each other? No person is an island, no one ever made it entirely on their own. Each person who succeeded in life did so because they stood on the shoulders of those who came before them, supported by the people who stood next to them. It's about changing the narrative from Us vs. Them to what can WE do for each other to make this world better for everyone?

Together we are strong, we are powerful and we can make our voices heard. If we can stop searching for our differences, and arguing over the fine details, we can find our common ground and become unstoppable. And that, more than anything is what those in power fear most. Not individuals divided by self-interest yelling at the sky, but of people united by a common goal, working together.

We will never agree 100% with any other human being, 100% of the time. We each have our own ideas, thoughts, and goals, but that does not mean we can't work together to bring about a better world for all of us. We the people deserve better than what we have been grudgingly given by those in power, giving us trinkets while they hoard the prizes that truly matter, life, liberty and the pursuit of happiness, safely cocooned by their power from the consequences of their actions that have made the majority of us miserable.

We are the change, we are the person we have been waiting for to do something. You may be thinking to yourself, I'm only one person, what can I do? You can change the world starting with one act of kindness, one good deed. Each time we stand up to be counted, when we refuse to be silent in the face of injustice, we make a difference. With each act, we build our army of revolutionaries, with the shared goal of a better world. We the People, united in our goals, moving forward through compromise, and compassion for others at the center of our movement, can become an unstoppable force.

IF I WERE DICTATOR

We have the power to change the world, the question is, will you?

With warmest regards,
Your retired Dictator,
Lisa

I'm so happy you made it all the way to the end :)

If you enjoyed this book, please consider leaving a review on GoodReads. You can use the QR code below to take you directly there.

ABOUT THE AUTHOR

Lisa Orban was born in Galesburg, IL a long time ago on a hot summer day. Due to various shenanigans by the adults in her life, her time in Galesburg was short and the family moved to Quincy, IL where they settled down for a good long stay.

Things were rolling along for a while inside the confines of Quincy, and Lisa rolled with them. There were several divorces, marriages, different schools, friends lost & gained, and many, *many* moves throughout all this activity. Until, quite unexpectedly, Lisa found herself in foster care at 16, much to her surprise.

Upon turning 18, Lisa ran away as fast as she could to Phoenix, AZ where she lived for 3 years. Got married, had a two sons, made many mistakes, and then eventually, ran for her life back to Quincy, where she still lives to this day.

Lisa went to college, earned an Associates in Psychology, raised her five kids, got married, and divorced, several times, bought a house and eventually settled down to live the life she always wanted, as the ringleader in a madhouse of anarchy. She now writes books, takes in strays in need of help, travels, opened a publishing house, and pretty much does whatever she wants, and is quite happy about it.

She became an author in 2015 with her first book, **It'll Feel Better when it Quits Hurting**, and hasn't stopped since. To find more books by Lisa, visit her page on Indies United using the QR code below.

www.ingramcontent.com/pod-product-compliance
Lightning Source LLC
Chambersburg PA
CBHW052026070526
44584CB00016B/1918